THE GOOD HEART BOOK

SO-AXP-062

A GUIDE TO VOLUNTEERING

DAVID E. DRIVER

The Noble Press, Inc.

Printed in the United States of America

Library of Congress Cataloging-in-Publication Data:
Driver, David E.
The good heart book: a guide to volunteering
David E. Driver
p. cm.
Includes bibliographic references
ISBN: 0-9622683-1-3 (pbk.) : $9.95
1. Voluntarism—United States.   2. Volunteer workers in social service—United States.   3. Social service—United States-Directories.   I. Title.
HN90.V64D75 1989
30.214'0973—cd 20   89-61442
CIP

Noble Press books are available in bulk at discount prices. Single copies are available prepaid direct from the publisher:

Marketing Director
The Noble Press, Inc.
213 W. Institute Pl., Suite 508
Chicago, IL 60610

Grateful acknowledgment is made for permission to reprint excepts from the following:

P.7, 52: Surveys from *Giving and Volunteering in the United States* reprinted with permission by INDEPENDENT SECTOR. P.17: Quotation reprinted with permission from Mary Scott Welch, *Ladies' Home Journal*, copyright 1979, Meredith Corporation. All rights reserved. P.21: Material from "Helper's High" by Allan Luks used with permission from *Psychology Today*, copyright 1989 (PT Partners, L.P.). P.47: "A Personal Inventory" reprinted with permission from United Way of Massachusetts Bay, Voluntary Action Center. P.72: "Rights and Responsibilities" by Marlene Wilson reprinted with permission from United Way of Massachusetts Bay, Voluntary Action Center. P.86, 87: Material from The New Homeless: Women, Children and Families, An Issues Forum on the Homeless used with permission by the Association of Junior Leagues, copyright 1988. P. 83: Material from "Deborah's Place," copyrighted, Chicago Tribune Company, all rights reserved. Used with permission. P.92: Quotation from "Really Cheap Eats" by Kristine F. Anderson, copyrighted Chicago Tribune, all rights reserved. Used with permission. P.92: "Volunteer Activities at the National Coalition for the Homeless" reprinted with permission by the New York Coalition for the Homeless. P.97: Quotation from "babies' Most Deadly Foe: Mom, Dad" by Patrick Reardon, copyrighted, Chicago Tribune Company, all rights reserved. Used with permission. P.98: Boarder Babies material used with permission by *U.S. News & World Report.* Copyright 1988. P.107: Material from sidebar used with permission by *U.S. News & World Report.* Copyright 1988. P.115: Material from "the Suburban Poor" used with permission by Newsweek, copyright 1989. P.129: Statistics used with permission, Coalition for Literacy. P.159: Sidebar material from "Women and AIDS: The Hidden Toll," by Mary Schmich and Jon Van. Copyrighted, Chicago Tribune Company, all rights reserved. Used with permission. P.172: Quotation used with permission from Little Friends, Inc.

*To everyone who has
ever extended a helping hand,
or needed one.*

CONTENTS

v

PREFACE

As the decade of the nineties begin, America's preoccupation with materialism, self-interest, and getting ahead at all cost appears to be abating. More and more, there are indications that people in large numbers are returning to more fundamental and fulfilling values, and showing a greater concern for their fellow man.

As a consequence of this self-interest and materialism, the 1980s have been a difficult period for many people. The number of poor, homeless, and disenfranchised citizens grew at unprecedented rates; even those who prospered found themselves spiritually empty and searching. I was among them.

Although I continued the volunteer work I had begun in college, my concern about the welfare of others fell far down on my priority list, well behind the attainment of things, career advancement, and peer approval. Like many others, my search for happiness and meaning through possessions and the approval of others left me asking the age old question: Is this all there is?

In recent years, I have rediscovered the spiritual enrichment that comes from being unselfishly involved with others, a reawakening to the fact that we receive what we need and desire not when we fervently seek it, but when we give.

I wrote this book because I believe that more and more people will be concerned about and interested in helping to improve the welfare of the less fortunate. And I also believe that the 1990s will be a healing period for us all as we come to realize that America is only as strong as its weakest citizen.

Through volunteering, all of us can establish our connection to our fellow man and do our part to strengthen the country. And in the process, we will become more fulfilled, spiritually healthy human beings.

ACKNOWLEDGMENTS

NO PROJECT is created in a vacuum, and this one is particularly indebted to the scores of volunteers and human care administrators who took the time and effort to tell us about their work, their ideals, and their lives. Their experiences and insights are at the heart of this book. John Mason, Winifred Brown, Christine Franklin, and Lynda Williams deserve particular thanks for their continual encouragement and support.

I would also like to thank Lisa Orkisz and Mary-Terese Cozzola for their work on this project, as well as the staff at The Noble Press: Mark Harris, Suzanne Roe, Eileen Lawrence, Dia Holman, Mary-Jean Beetel, and Blanche Lang for their help in turning an idea into a reality.

PART I

Becoming A Volunteer

CHAPTER ONE

A Call to Volunteering

E VERY SATURDAY morning David Mueller leaves his suit and tie in the closet and puts on a pair of ragged blue jeans and beaten up tennis shoes. Then he takes off, not to his law office downtown, but to a much less glamorous section of Chicago, the near Westside. There he joins other volunteers, lost in a cloud of sawdust and noise, in renovating a dilapidated house which will soon be home for a low-income family. David, age thirty, has continually been confronted with evidence of the lack of available housing for the poor. "You can't live in the city and not see the homeless problem," he says. "You can't even walk through a single block downtown without seeing several homeless people. Sometimes the city seems like it's Calcutta or something!" Although he had done some volunteer work at a local shelter, it wasn't until David heard a speaker affiliated with Habitat for Humanity that he realized he could do something tangible, something physical, that would help to solve the housing problem. He accepted the speaker's challenge to get involved, and now as the Habitat house nears completion, David takes satisfaction in having helped rebuild a house for a family which otherwise would never have owned one. "It's very gratifying," he says, "to create something that's tangible, with results that you can see."

A Ph.D. student in English Literature, Ann spends most of her time in the library working on her dissertation on 18th-century theories of the picturesque. But once a week she deals with more contemporary concerns by visiting a homebound eighty-nine-year-old woman. "I got involved with Neighbors Helping Neighbors," says Ann, "because I felt I wasn't giving anything to anyone. I work so much by myself on abstract things that I felt I needed to do something that would connect me with

3

the world and that would do some concrete good." When she saw a sign in her neighborhood asking her *Can You Give One Hour A Week To An Elderly Person?* she saw a chance to make that connection. During their weekly visits, she and Agnes go shopping, look at old pictures and magazines, or just talk. Ann enjoys the time they spend together. "I like talking to Agnes. She's interesting, and I'm able to clear my head by telling her what's going on in my life."

When asked her age, Toni tells you she is a "great grandmother." But at a time of life when most people sit back and enjoy their well-deserved retirement, she is busier as a volunteer than she has ever been—and more active than those a third her age. When not working at her part-time job with the Convention and Tourism Bureau, Toni volunteers as a nurse's assistant at a Hospice and AIDS unit, as a counselor at a battered women's shelter and a hotline for runaway teenagers, and as a cook at a homeless shelter. Of all this volunteer work, she says simply, "I just like to help people, because everyone needs a hand once in a while." And age has not prevented her from extending that hand. "I don't care if you're five or fifty or seventy or a hundred, you can do something. You can always do something for someone. Age is a state of mind. I'm not old, I'm just getting older."

Although they come from very different backgrounds, David, Ann and Toni have one thing in common: they are part of a growing segment of the population which is volunteering its time and energy to help others. Bored with the materialism of the 1980s and moved into action by an increased awareness of the seriousness of our country's social problems, more and more Americans are becoming personally involved in helping to improve the lives of the less fortunate.

This growing involvement of Americans in social and political concerns is a sign that the country is moving into a new period of progress and enlightenment. In the past, it has been during times like these when America has made tremendous strides in achieving equal opportunity, improving economic and political fairness and the health and living conditions for all of its citizens. We can now look ahead to a time of similar prosperity and social progress.

Confirmation of American's increasing social involvement

and changing values was provided by the 1990 Gallup Poll which surveyed American attitudes toward charity and volunteering. The study showed that charitable giving in 1989 soared from its 1987 level, led by large increases in giving by baby boomers, the affluent, and African-Americans. In fact, 19% of those surveyed said they had given to a charity for the first time during the previous year. Health, education, environmental, and youth organizations were the charities that benefited most from the increase in contributions.

The Gallup Poll also showed large increases in regular church attendance and in the number of Americans doing volunteer work. According to the study, weekly church attendance increased from 29% in 1987 to 37% in 1989. Because of the strong correlation between church attendance and volunteering, it's not surprising that the number of people volunteering also rose dramatically, up 23% from the 1987 level. In 1989, an estimated 54% of adult Americans, over ninety-eight million people, were engaged in some type of volunteer work.

These increases in volunteerism and charitable giving were not limited to just social causes. Americans are also increasingly pitching in to help improve the environment and to work for political causes they believe in. The number of people who give to environmental organizations and who express concern for the environment has grown tremendously. In addition, more and more Americans are advocating for political issues they believe in. Whether the issue is tax fairness, war, equal opportunity, or abortion, the number of Americans who are attending rallies, writing letters and volunteering for political causes is on the rise.

This growing social and political awareness has prompted action from governmental and corporate leaders alike. President Bush's 1,000 Points of Light program and Senator Edward Kennedy's National and Community Service Act encourage and support social and environmental volunteerism. What is especially significant about these programs is their focus on the nation's youth. The programs encourage elementary and secondary schools to incorporate community service into their curricula. They have also established The Youth Service Corps to encourage young people to work in government agencies, day-care centers, nursing homes and other nonprofit institutions. The National and Community Service Act also has an environmental component, the American Conservation Corps, to encourage volunteerism in our nation's parks and recreational areas. Corporations are also responding by providing increased volunteer opportunities for their employees. According to one source, since 1984 the number of corporate-sponsored volunteer programs has doubled to 1,200.

As a result of these social, environmental and political volunteer movements, the severity of the problems currently facing our society will be lessened. Through the efforts of volunteers, the number of Americans who are considered unfortunate can be reduced. The health of our environment will be improved, while our political system will become one that is truly fair and that adequately represents Americans from all walks of life.

While for many this interest in social and political volunteerism may seem new, it is actually as old as America itself. It was volunteers who laid the foundation for this country almost four hundred years ago. Volunteers on both sides supported the soldiers during the Civil War. It was volunteers who led the fight for child labor laws and women's right to vote in the early 1900s, and who won gains for the poor, minorities and women in the 1960s. Indeed, throughout history, it has been the involvement of volunteers in important causes that have propelled America forward.

What has also been true historically, and is still very true today, is the positive impact volunteerism has on those who participate. Those men, women and teens who give of themselves to improve the lives of others receive much in return. The feeling of purpose that comes from being involved in a cause that is bigger than oneself, and the self-respect that comes from unselfishness are among the volunteer's many rewards. The rewards from volunteering were best described by Ralph Waldo Emerson when he wrote:

> It is one of the most beautiful compensations in life that no man can help another without helping himself.

GUIDE FOR VOLUNTEERS

Whether you are a seasoned volunteer or someone long interested in becoming one, *The Good Heart Book* is for you. It has been written to serve as a complete guide to human care volunteering. For the beginner, Part I provides a step-by-step plan for getting involved in volunteering. This section answers the questions most commonly asked by prospective volunteers: Which volunteer organization should I join? What will be expected of me?

WHO VOLUNTEERS?
The 1990 Volunteering Survey

Estimated number of Americans who volunteer:		98.4 million
Volunteers who give five or more hours per week:		25.6 million
Percentage of each sex that volunteers:		
	Male	52%
	Female	56%
Percentage of age groups that volunteer:		
	18–24	43%
	25–34	62%
	35–44	64%
	45–54	56%
	55–64	51%
	65–74	47%
	74+	32%
Percentage of people who volunteer by income:		
	$10,000–	30%
	10–19,000	42%
	20–29,000	56%
	30–39,000	64%
	40–49,000	67%
	50–74,000	62%
	75–99,000	62%
	$100,000+	73%
Percentage of people who volunteer by racial group:		
	White	57%
	Black	38%
	Hispanic	36%

Statistics taken from the 1990 Gallup Organization National Survey, *Giving and Volunteering in the United States*. The survey was commissioned by INDEPENDENT SECTOR.

Who do I contact? How do I fit volunteering into my busy life-style? For the experienced volunteer, it provides valuable information on how to maintain the volunteer spirit and how to become a more effective volunteer.

Part II focuses on particular social problems volunteers may want to become involved in, such as homelessness, battered women, inner-city poverty, AIDS, teenagers in crisis, illiteracy, abused children, the elderly and people with disabilities. Each chapter is devoted to one of these problem areas and examines the issues involved. Each looks at what is being done to alleviate the problem and how volunteers can best help. Part II also profiles a variety of volunteers and social service professionals to give you an insider's view of the volunteer experience, looking at both its rewards and its difficulties.

Part III is a national directory of social service organizations and volunteer referral agencies. Addresses and phone numbers are included so that anyone interested in volunteering or learning more about the organizations can easily contact them.

AMERICANS IN NEED

It is a sad irony that in this wealthy country a large percentage of the population lives in misery. Poverty, homelessness, malnutrition, illiteracy, and family violence affect millions of Americans every day. On the surface, however, things have never looked better. During the 1980s, America enjoyed the longest period of economic expansion in its history. The numbers of millionaires and corporate profits were at all-time highs. Prosperity abounded. At least that's the way it looked at the top. At the bottom, however, it was a much different story. During that same ten-year period the number of people living in poverty and without shelter or adequate health care increased dramatically. People died from malnutrition, AIDS, substance abuse, and family violence at unprecedented rates. A look at some of the latest statistics reveals the seriousness of these social problems.

Poverty

The number of Americans whose household earnings fall below the poverty line has grown by seven million since 1979, an increase of 27%. Many of the poor are children. One out of every five children lives in poverty, many belonging to welfare families headed by females. These families have been disproportionately affected by the high inflation of the last twenty years. A recent study by the Center on Budget and Policy Priorities found that in many states the buying power of public aid has fallen by more than 50% since 1970.

Illiteracy and Education

Twenty-seven million Americans over the age of eighteen, nearly 15% of the adult population, can neither read nor write. The nation's high school drop-out rate stands at 25%, with the rate in some inner-city schools surpassing 50%.

Family Violence

The increase in the number of reported cases of child and spouse abuse is alarming. A recent study on family violence estimated the number of battered women and children to be as high as three million. Another study conducted by The National Committee for the Prevention of Child Abuse reported that in 1986 at least 1,300 children died from parental abuse.

Homelessness

The National Coalition for the Homeless estimates that at least three million Americans are homeless, a number that is growing. Over half a million children are homeless. The decreasing supply of low-income housing and shortage of shelters and missions force many of these people to sleep in alleyways, train stations and city parks.

Malnutrition and Health Care

While the world's attention is fixed on the people starving in Africa, children are dying every day in America from malnutrition. The Greater Chicago Food Depository reports that in Chicago two or more children die daily from the effects of malnutrition. Another ten die weekly due to inadequate maternal nutrition. The nation's poor, already weakened by improper diets, are the least likely to receive adequate health care. A decrease in federal government funding for health care has resulted in a reduction in the number of hospitals and physicians willing to treat the poor. More and more doctors are refusing Medicaid and public aid patients due to low reimbursements. This situation is aggravated by the number of hospitals serving the poor that have closed since 1980.

Suicide

During the last decade suicides among teenagers have tripled: every day, more than 1,000 teens will attempt to kill themselves. The problem is not isolated to the young, however; it is just as big a problem among the elderly population. Senior citizens, who represent only 11% of the nation's total population, account for 25% of all suicides. Many people in both of these age groups are desperately crying out for help.

What is most disturbing about all of these statistics is that they reveal an increasing trend: the number of people in this country living in some type of crisis situation is growing at an alarming rate. In fact, many of these situations have long since surpassed epidemic proportions. In light of the above statistics, we must ask ourselves how America can be considered truly prosperous when so many of its citizens are suffering.

VOLUNTEER CHALLENGES IN THE NINETIES

What is also disturbing about the enormous increase in the number of disadvantaged people during the 1980s is that it occurred during a time when over eighty million Americans — almost half the adult population—were doing volunteer work. While this dichotomy might lead some skeptics to suggest that volunteerism does not work, the real explanation is much more complex.

During the eighties, volunteers and social service professionals fought an uphill battle to help the victims of the Reagan administration's conservative policies. These policies, masked in catchy phrases such as *trickle-down economics, deregulation, reverse discrimination,* and *tax reform,* placed a serious financial burden on the already beleaguered poor, minorities, and working class.

America's working class was financially devastated by the loss of 11.5 million manufacturing jobs during the decade. Spurred on by deregulation and the weakening of unions and worker protection laws, corporations shipped production capacity overseas, shut plants, and shifted assets from production to leveraged buyouts. The resulting unemployment caused many of the working class to fall below the poverty line.

And while the cutbacks in environmental, worker safety, and consumer protection standards, and the reduction in social, educational, and health programs negatively impacted all Americans, those most seriously devastated were the poor, minorities,

FIRST TIME JITTERS

Eileen stood outside the Ulrich Children's Home trying to calm the butterflies in her stomach. Although the Ulrich staff members had seemed friendly and supportive, Eileen's nervousness about the kids and how they would respond to her just wouldn't go away.

Eileen, who grew up in a middle-class suburb of Chicago, knew that the background of the children who lived at Ulrich was vastly different from hers. Most of the kids were from violent, poverty stricken homes. They had either been abandoned or removed from their homes by the state because they had been abused. "How could I relate to them or they to me? I could not even imagine what these kids have been through," Eileen thought.

Eileen's greatest fear, however, was that the kids would reject her because of the differences in background. "I really worried about that, but I had made a commitment. So I took a deep breath, and walked through the front door to begin my volunteer experience."

As she entered the office of the volunteer administrator, Barb Gill, Eileen noticed three girls, ages eight to twelve, lobbying Barb for a spot on the new Ulrich cheerleading squad. As Eileen walked in, Barb said, "Don't ask me, talk to your new coach about it." The three girls, with big eyes and even bigger smiles, turned and begin showering Eileen with compliments and petitions for a chance to be a cheerleader.

With three new friends, Eileen waved to Barb as the girls lead her off to the gym to meet the rest of the future squad. When Barb shouted to Eileen, "You ready for this, kid?," Eileen noticed for the first time that her butterflies had disappeared. She turned to Barb smiling and said, "Sure. Piece of cake."

the elderly, and people with disabilities. No social programs were exempt from the conservative ax: social security, education, Medicare, food stamps, student loans, welfare, school lunches, job training, unemployment benefits, disability programs, and programs to foster equal rights for minorities and women.

As a result of these cutbacks, the number of people living in poverty increased by seven million. The number of homeless reached an estimated three million people, while the number of illiterate Americans reached twenty-seven million. In fact, there were so many destitute Americans with so little hope of recovery that sociologists created a new term to describe them—the underclass.

According to the conservative policy makers, the increase in the poor and disadvantaged Americans should not have occurred. For years they had preached the trickle-down theory, in which prosperity would "trickle down" to the less fortunate. Despite their claims however, the eighties witnessed the greatest shift of wealth from the poor to the wealthiest 20% of the population since the Census Bureau began keeping statistics in 1946. This shift of wealth was mostly due to large tax cuts for the wealthy, financed by the 34% reduction in spending on social programs.

The irony of all this is that many Americans who considered themselves sympathetic towards the disadvantaged — including many of the eighty million volunteers and some social service professionals — openly embraced the conservative policies of the eighties. Either consumed by the opportunity for self-gain, or attracted to moral issues such as abortion or school prayer, or simply confused by fancy political rhetoric, kindhearted American elected and reelected those whose ideals are contrary, even deadly, to the millions of disadvantaged children and their families.

Herein lies the explanation for the dichotomy between the high level of public interest in improving the lives of the disadvantaged (as evidenced in the growing number of volunteers) and the fact that the plight of the disadvantaged has worsened. While Americans were giving a helping hand to those in need, they were at the same time supporting public policies that were extremely detrimental to those they were helping.

"You Can't Hire Love"

While hosting a White House luncheon in its honor, Barbara Bush spoke of the special service performed by Family Friends. "I can't imagine and program that better exemplifies all the things George Bush talks about when he talks about a kinder, gentler nation." Mrs. Bush was honoring this volunteer group for its work in improving the lives of children with disabilities and their families.

Family Friends works to alleviate some of the special burdens faced by families of children with exceptional needs. Children with disabilities or severe illnesses often require constant care, and the resulting demands on their families can cause severe physical, emotional, and financial stress. Family Friends, whose volunteers range in age from fifty-five to eighty-five years old, helps to alleviate that stress by sharing their time and love.

The volunteers are trained by medical and social service professionals to assist with the care of special needs children. After training, they spend several hours or more each week assisting the family in caring for the disabled child.

"The volunteer and the family usually develop a very close relationship," says Lynda Williams, who is the Director of Program Development for the Washington, D.C. Family Friends. "The volunteer provides the parents with much needed support, someone to talk to who understands the difficulty of caring for a special needs child." Says Williams, "Sometimes what the parent really needs is a break, someone to take over for a few hours so they can have some time to themselves."

As the pilot program, the Washington, D.C. Family Friends is somewhat unique. Its primary focus has been on families living in the heart of the District of Columbia. For these parents who are raising their families in a tough inner-city environment, the additional burden of caring for a child with special needs is especially trying.

"What really excites me about this program," says Williams, "is seeing the volunteers having such a profound effect on the lives of the families, and the families having such a positive impact on the volunteers."

In Washington, D.C. and seven other cities, the senior volunteers of Family Friends are helping people manage under difficult circumstances. Currently working to develop a national umbrella network, Family Friends will be expanding to other cities across the country.

The Family Friends program is well represented by its motto, "You can't hire love." You cannot pay for what these volunteers give: their love and support come from being part of the family.

Fortunately, the Bush administration is more sensitive to the needs of the segment of the population that is disadvantaged. Barbara Bush has become the country's leading spokesperson in the campaign against illiteracy, and President Bush has established a White House task force to find solutions to poverty. And most importantly, the President's Points of Light Foundation is embarking on an ambitious campaign to "make direct and consequential community services aimed at serious social problems central to the life of every American."

But still, today's volunteers will have to redouble their efforts if they want to prevent the problems of the 1980s from reoccurring in the 1990s. In addition to volunteering a couple of hours a week, they will also have to embrace the concerns and interests of those they serve. Volunteers can no longer be silent about governmental and public indifference toward the needy. They must speak up, with their voices and voting power, so that their family and friends will also understand the plight of the disadvantaged. Volunteers must let corporate and political leaders know that there are over eighty million Americans who care about those in need.

Together, a voice and a helping hand, will make the difference. Through these, the neglect of the eighties can be reversed, and America can again move toward equality and economic fairness for all.

CHAPTER TWO

The Joy of Service

A S I DROVE to my speaking engagement with the Retired Senior Volunteers of Wisconsin's Waukesha County, I felt uneasy about how the audience would respond to my ideas on volunteerism and social policy. I had assumed that the audience was probably very conservative, very reserved, and very critical. I had never met any of these people before, but because they were over sixty-five years of age and lived in a conservative county in Wisconsin, I thought I had a pretty good idea of what this group would be like.

But my perceptions were shaken the moment I walked into the meeting room. The loud buzz of conversation and laughter filled the room with high energy. This group of so-called "senior citizens" was having a party. As I spoke to some them of them individually, we swapped "war stories" about our most memorable or humorous volunteer experiences. We talked about travel, politics, and food. After an hour of socializing, I felt a kinship with these volunteers, despite the differences in our ages and backgrounds.

When it came time for me to speak, my new friends were cheering me on. After the applause and jokes died down, I looked around the room at this group of healthy, smiling, and playful senior citizens. At that moment, I realized that this group of volunteers had come to define for me what the phrase, "the joy of service" really meant.

There are millions of volunteers like the Retired Seniors of Waukesha County who have discovered the real joy that comes from helping others in need. And perhaps that is the greatest irony about volunteering — that helping others, frequently in depressing or disturbing situations, benefits the volunteer as much as it does those being helped. Indeed, in talking to volunteers across the country, we have found that their volunteer experiences have significantly contributed to making them feel happier and better about themselves. As one volunteer who has worked in a number of organizations said, "It makes you feel better about your whole life."

Volunteering can provide a host of other benefits in addition to joy, including new friends, new skills, increased self confidence, and a different perspective on and understanding of life. Ultimately, volunteering leads you to discover more about yourself.

This chapter will help you to better understand the "joy of service." You will know what people really mean when they say that volunteering makes them "feel better" and gives them a sense of fulfillment. It will explain the relationship between volunteering and psychology, health, and religion, and give you examples of the many tangible benefits volunteers receive, such as new skills and friends. You will see how volunteering has made life more enjoyable and meaningful for the many people who have made that commitment to help others.

SELF-FULFILLMENT THROUGH VOLUNTEERING

When asked why she volunteers, Ashley, a research assistant at the National institute of Mental Health says, "It's probably because I really enjoy the satisfaction that I get out of it. You know, feeling like you are doing something good is a rewarding experience. It makes you feel good about yourself."

The positive feelings Ashley gets from volunteering are not unique. Statements such as "it makes me feel happier" and "it makes me feel better about myself" are repeated again and again in surveys conducted by researchers studying volunteerism. These surveys show that people volunteer not only because they want to help others, but also because volunteering makes them feel useful, needed and fulfilled. In effect, Ashley and other volunteers receive from helping others what many Americans in the eighties were trying to achieve through preoccupation with self-satisfaction and materialism—peace and happiness.

During the eighties, self-interest was in vogue. By the end of the decade, the casualties were everywhere: the country's financial system lay severely damaged by greed; corrupt businessmen, judges, politicians, and even religious leaders, were in prison; the family unit, once the stabilizing force in America, was seriously impaired by a decade of neglect.

And what about those who benefited financially from the eighties? Perhaps they are part of the millions of Americans who bought self-help books in record numbers, looking to attain the happiness missing from their lives. Or perhaps they are part of the fifteen million Americans who joined self-help groups during the last decade, seeking relief from the emptiness and pain that comes from self-centeredness. These groups treat a variety of ailments, from chemical abuse to anxiety, but in the end it's inner-peace their members want most.

"It's What You Become"

After a lifetime of social service, Winifred Brown has seen the lives of many volunteers changed by their volunteer service. "After you spend several months working with homeless people or babies born with AIDS, you're not the same person you were when you started," she says.

As executive director of the Mayor's Voluntary Action Center, Brown and her organization have received numerous presidential citations and awards for the programs they have initiated to combat homelessness, youth unemployment, and AIDS in New York City.

In the last few years, Brown has watched new groups of young professionals, like New York Cares and The Street Project, being formed to promote volunteerism among their peers. "Many young people join these groups for altruistic and social reasons. But what they soon find is how volunteering changes them as a person," says Brown. "They become more sensitive, more caring, more realistic about the world around them. They find that volunteering is a learning, growing experience."

In spite of all the benefits volunteers receive from their service work, Brown believes there is something more important. To make her point, she quotes Journalist Mary Scott Welch: "It is not what you get from volunteer work or even what you give, it's what you become."

The philosopher Thomas Merton understood our desire for inner-peace and happiness, but he also realized that real, lasting happiness does not result from a selfish pursuit of it. In *No Man is An Island*, Merton writes:

> A happiness that is sought for ourselves alone can never be found: for a happiness that is diminished by being shared is not big enough to make us happy.

There is a false and momentary happiness in self-satisfaction, but it always leads to sorrow because it narrows and deadens our spirit. True happiness is found in unselfish love.

Because the desire to volunteer emanates from unselfishness and compassion, many therapists, counselors, and self-help programs are recommending volunteer work as one of the ways people can find happiness in their lives. In fact, twelve-step self-help groups encourage their members to reach out to help others as one of the steps to emotional and spiritual recovery.

While there are many ways for people to show concern and share with others, volunteer work is unique in its ability to help us learn and develop new, unselfish thoughts and behaviors; meet our human needs in a positive way; and contribute to a healthy self-esteem.

It is one thing to realize that our thoughts and behaviors contribute to our unhappiness, but it's quite another to change them. Years of habitual behavior, such as self-centeredness, cannot be cured through awareness alone; it requires *new* actions and new thoughts. Volunteering allows us, on a regular basis, to give to others without asking for anything in return. At first, this may feel strange, especially for those who suffer from self-centeredness, insecurity, ego-mania, co-dependency, and over ambition. But over time, due to the positive reinforcements you will no doubt receive from volunteering, it will become a new and refreshing habit.

One of the other wonderful attributes of volunteer work is how it meets some of our human needs. In *The Theory of Human Motivation*, Dr. Abraham Maslow stresses how important loving, being loved, and feeling needed are to our emotional well-being. We can see the truth in Maslow's theory when we think about the lengths we have gone to receive love or to feel needed by our families, friends, and co-workers. Helping others gives us an opportunity to both give and receive the love we all need.

Finally, one of the most valuable benefits of volunteering is the positive impact it has on one's self-respect. Low self-esteem is considered the root cause of much of the emotional stress and unhappiness we feel today. Growing up in a Judeo-Christian society, we are taught moral values and personal ethics. We come to believe that principles such as loving others, giving, and honesty are positive values, while selfishness, hoarding and dishonesty are not. These beliefs come to define our personal value system, the way we judge others and ourselves. For example, most of us have tremendous respect for Mother Teresa or Dr. Martin Luther King Jr., while we view Adolph Hitler or Saddam Hussein as evil. Would we not respect ourselves more if we lived more in concert with our values, if we lived more like Mother Theresa? Volunteering gives us an opportunity to put some of our values and beliefs into action, which in turn increases our self-respect.

Peace and happiness—these are the reasons volunteering is so important to millions of Americans. It provides us an opportu-

Volunteering to Find Fulfillment

It's easy to see why Pat Keen, director of the Westside Chicago Habitat for Humanity, is so popular with the workers at the project site. A jovial man with a booming bass voice and a hearty and frequent laugh, Pat walks around the noisy and dusty site keeping spirits high —encouraging, congratulating, and joking with the volunteers. By the end of the shift, there is not one person he hasn't talked to at least briefly. Part of his popularity stems from the fact that he seems to understand the volunteers and their decision to build homes for the poor.

"I think people volunteer because it's fulfilling," he says. "It fulfills a need we have within ourselves to contribute more to solving the problems of the work. People see volunteering as an opportunity to make a difference in their corner of the world. They volunteer at the Habitat projects because they are not just sending their money and saying someone else will do it. They are coming to make a difference themselves, so that they can stand back and say, 'This is what I've done today. This is what I've done this week.' There's a sense of pride, and they feel a sense of fulfillment within themselves for what they have done."

nity to be part of something bigger and inherently more important than our own little worlds; it gives a richer meaning to our lives. Volunteering reinforces the true meaning of love; it reins in our tendencies toward the spiritually self-draining patterns of selfishness and self-interest. Given these tremendous benefits that volunteers reap, it's not surprising that those who volunteer are healthier and happier than those who do not.

HEALTH AND VOLUNTEERING

A number of people interviewed for this book indicated that volunteering helped them relieve some of the stress they felt in their jobs and day-to-day lives. Although Susan enjoys her work in the public defender's office, she sees her time as a volunteer with young children as a way of keeping a balance in her life. "I'm around heavy people all the time," she says, "but then I get around those kids and it's so light." For Ann, who is working on her Ph.D., volunteering is likewise an opportunity to "clear [her] head."

Many physicians feel that "unmanaged" stress is a contributor to numerous physical and psychological illnesses. One national study found that 82% of the people surveyed needed to reduce the stress in their lives in order to improve their health.

Researchers have recently begun studying volunteering as a way of reducing that stress. One survey shows that many of the volunteers studied experienced a greater calm and enhanced self-worth after volunteering. This "helper's calm" appears to be related to reduced emotional stress. The researchers also discovered that almost three-quarters of the volunteers reported feeling an identifiable physical sensation when volunteering that was comparable to the stimulation they received when exercising or playing sports. Allan Luks, executive director of the Institute for the Advancement of Health, has described this physical sensation as a "helper's high."

While a number of national surveys have found that volunteers tend to be healthier and happier than others their own age, one study even suggests that volunteerism contributes to a longer life. Researchers studied 2,700 older men in Tecumseh, Michigan over a ten-year period. At the end of the study, they found that the men who were not involved in volunteer work were two-and-a-half times more likely to die during the study period that those who were actively volunteering.

Volunteering can also be useful in reducing the amount of stress and frustration in your life. Helping others with "real" problems and major life crises allows you to put your own problems in perspective. After counseling an abused child or working with people who don't have adequate shelter or enough food, your own problems don't seem to be as major as they once appeared.

In addition, volunteering is especially helpful in reducing the frustrations caused by our occupations. Many of the problems people have with their careers stem from a lack of psychological fulfillment. People today expect their jobs to provide them not only with financial rewards, but with enhanced self-esteem and

---

"Helper's High"

"Sometimes I get a real 'rush' when I feel like I made a breakthrough with one of the kids. But for the most part, I get a warm feeling all over," says John, a volunteer at a shelter for runaway teens. John was attempting to describe how he felt during and after his volunteer work. Allan Luks, executive director of the Institute for the Advancement of Health, has characterized this rush and subsequent feelings of warmth as a "helper's high."

In an article in *Psychology Today,* Luks describes the identifiable physical sensations felt by volunteers surveyed by the Institute. Over 70% of those polled reported feeling one or more of the following sensations when volunteering:

High	52%
Stronger, more energetic	44%
Warm	27%
Calmer, less depressed	25%
A greater feeling of self-worth	21%
Fewer aches and pains	14%

Several volunteers described the sensations they felt from helping to be similar to those they got when playing sports. Unlike with sports, however, most volunteers surveyed said their sensations would reoccur when they recalled their helping experience.

Reprinted with permission from *Psychology Today,* copyright 1989 (PT Partners, L.P.).

feelings of belonging and accomplishment as well. When these expectations are not being met, a worker becomes increasingly disenchanted, perhaps changing jobs as a result. But that does not change the real problem. A better solution may be to become involved in other activities that provide the needed psychological benefits.

Volunteering is helpful in these circumstances because it provides an unique opportunity to gain the needed psychological benefits missing from your career. Anita Katz, director of an organization that pairs young people with the elderly, suggests that in choosing a volunteer job you consider those things missing in your career and look to gain them in your volunteer work. In meeting some of your personal needs through volunteering, you may remove some of the unreal expectations you have placed on your career, making your work less frustrating and stressful.

TANGIBLE BENEFITS

Outside of the good feeling that comes from helping someone in need or working to improve a situation, most people don't think about the benefits to be gained from volunteering. But once involved, many have found that their volunteer experience has helped them in areas they never imagined when they first signed up. Listed below are some of these benefits:

New Skills

Volunteers naturally develop new skills, which vary depending on the nature of their work. Most mention increased human relations and communication ability, but many talk of specific skills learned on the job, such as crisis counseling, public relations, and even first aid.

Most of the workers at a Habitat for Humanity project in Chicago talked about the new carpentry skills they picked up at the site. One dock worker was looking to gain some experience on the project before starting on his own house. "I'm learning how to drywall," he said. "I already know something about electricity, but I could use some help on plumbing. I'm picking up carpentry and construction pretty well."

New Friends

Almost all volunteers interviewed talked about the new friends they had made. They also commented on the type of people they met while volunteering, kind, sincere people who often share the same concerns and priorities in life.

David, an attorney, talked about the "camaraderie" and the chance "to get to know people" in other parts of the city. Pearl, who works with kids in an early intervention program, said that at times, "I feel bad that I enjoy myself so much" because she can "meet so many people and make so many friends."

What was most surprising however, were the number of married volunteers who indicated they had met their spouse while volunteering together.

New Outlooks

Working as a volunteer will give you a new and informed perspective on social problems.

Karen says her work at a shelter for battered women has made her aware of "the extent of real domestic violence that people live with in this society."

After working with a homeless man and teaching him how to read, Laura saw the reality of the homeless problem. "You know there are [homeless] people out there, but a lot of people ignore it." Laura's perspective on homelessness and poverty changed after she got involved.

As a volunteer visiting and counseling jailed prostitutes, Lori says she has learned a lot about the "ugly realities of prostitution," as well as a great deal about general urban problems and the court system—an education she claims has made her more "realistic."

Career Benefits

A number of volunteers commented on how their professional lives had benefited through their volunteer work. Some gained valuable experience they were able to use on their jobs. Others talked about how their volunteer work strengthened their resumes, while others commented on valuable business contacts they had made while volunteering.

In New York, The Street Project offers an informal network of contacts for volunteers who work on Wall Street. At IBM, serving on projects like the Faculty Loan Program or the Community Service Assignment Program allows volunteers to gain a higher level of friendship with and understanding of co-workers.

Susan's volunteer work as a tutor to Native Americans has helped her become a better lawyer. "With adults," she says, "you don't have to explain yourself as clearly as you do to a child. As a lawyer, I've realized how important my communication skills are."

Personal Insight

The many people we talked to claimed that their volunteer work not only gave them the opportunity to observe the lifestyles of others, but also to reflect on their own.

John, a stock broker, says volunteering has made him "more aware of [my] excesses and frivolous spending," in addition to helping him "de-emphasize materialism and to appreciate how very fortunate" he is.

Lori's work with prostitutes has given her perspective on the uncertainties of life. "I've really realized how fragile everybody's life is."

Group Volunteering

The benefits of volunteering are not limited to individuals, however. Volunteering also benefits groups, creating and strengthening bonds between members and increasing a sense of unity and purpose. A family can adopt a children's shelter, for instance. Not only will the common goals bring the family closer together, but their children will learn a valuable lesson in how to share with others.

People who work together in an office or factory, attend the same church, or are in the same class at school, can come together through volunteering. Bob began his volunteering through the IBM corporate volunteer program. Since then he has grown closer to many fellow IBM volunteers he would have not met otherwise. Many local churches and schools have adopted volunteer programs at homeless missions or food depositories. Group volunteering not only offers all the benefits of service work, but it also builds camaraderie and respect between members of the group.

LOVE, RELIGION AND VOLUNTEERING

"Faith in action is love, and love in action is service, and proof of action is peace." These words, written by Mother Teresa, show us from where the greatest joy from volunteer work emanates — from the peace we receive when we are living in concert with God's commandment, "Love thy neighbor as thyself."

The act of loving one's neighbor is taught and exemplified in all major religions. The Spiritual leader Dalai Lama wrote "Kindness is my true religion. The essence of all religion is love, compassion and tolerance." This is also true of Judaism, in which the believer is taught to go beyond just giving to the disadvantaged. Sab.63a says, "Moreover, of greater merit than giving to the poor, is to help him to become self-supporting."

Christianity, however, provides us with the greatest example of charity, the life of Jesus Christ. His life here on earth was de-

---

Christ and Charity

Readers familiar with the New Testament may recognize the story of Christ describing to his apostles the importance placed on charity by his Father in Heaven.

"Then the King will say to the people on the right, 'Come you blessed of my father! Come and inherit the kingdom prepared for you from the creation of the world. For when I was hungry, you gave me food; I was thirsty and you gave me drink; I was a stranger and you took me in; I was naked and you clothed me; I was sick and you visited me; I was in prison and you came to see me.'

Then the righteous will answer him saying, 'Lord, when did we see you hungry and feed you, or thirsty and gave you drink? When did we see you a stranger, naked or in prison? When did we see you sick and visited you?'

And the King will answer and say to them, 'assuredly, I say to you, in as much as you did it to one of the least of the brethren, you did it to me."

Matthew 25:31-40

voted to teaching and helping the less fortunate of his day. For Christian believers peace is found by living their life like Christ did—sharing themselves with those in need.

The love that the religious community has shown for its fellow man has been one of the driving forces behind America's volunteer spirit. Whether large organizations such as Catholic Charities, the Salvation Army, or the Council of Jewish Women, or smaller groups such as local synagogues or churches, religious institutions play a major role in providing human care services to the needy.

The church's involvement in volunteering has not only helped the disadvantaged, but has brought tremendous benefits to the church as well. Volunteering strengthens the faith and camaraderie among the members of the church. Pat Keen, director of a local Habitat For Humanity housing branch, has seen it happen on his project. "A number of congregations come out every Saturday, a heck of a commitment," Pat says, "But I've had pastors respond to me that they have seen a change in their congregation as a result of it. The giving to the church increases, communication between the members increases, all because they're working here trying to get to know each other better."

The biggest benefactors however, are the church members themselves. Volunteering gives them the opportunity to put into action the love they feel for their fellow man. For the Christian, it is an opportunity to live like Christ did. For members of other religions, it is an opportunity to follow the examples provided by the leaders of their faith. This, as Mother Teresa reminds us, is what leads to peace.

CHAPTER THREE

Human Care Organizations

O NE OF THE most exciting aspects of volunteering is the freedom of choice it provides the volunteer. As a volunteer, you can choose to work in many different areas of social concerns, in hundreds of volunteer job descriptions and in thousands of different organizations interested in utilizing your services.

To use your freedom of choice wisely, however, it helps to have some knowledge of the types of organizations and volunteer jobs available. The type of organization or job you choose will have an enormous impact on the degree to which you enjoy and benefit from volunteering. In fact, many veteran volunteers were amazed at how working in one organization versus another impacted on how much they enjoyed their work.

This chapter will help you make an informed decision about which volunteer organization or job is best for you. It will give you information about the different types of volunteer organizations that are out there and what volunteer jobs are available, and on the different types of management structures and volunteer policies and how they will influence your work.

TYPES OF ORGANIZATIONS

There are hundreds of thousands of voluntary organizations in operation across America. Each has its own special mission and has developed a structure and operating philosophy to best deliver its message and services to its clientele. As a group, however, they can be loosely divided into categories according to their functions. Among these general categories are:

Umbrella Groups

Umbrella groups are primarily national non-profit organizations that promote volunteerism, raise funds, and provide information and administrative support to other voluntary organizations. Since the primary function of umbrella organizations is administrative in nature, their volunteer needs are for people skilled in public relations, management, accounting, fundraising and administration. Examples of umbrella organizations include ACTION, National Center for Voluntary Action, INDEPENDENT SECTOR, United Way of America, and VOLUNTEER— The National Center.

The Salvation Army: Fighting For The Needy

If William Booth had been too busy to edit the galleys of his group's 1878 annual report, today we would be calling The Salvation Army The Hallelujah Army. That's what Booth's band of converted prostitutes, gamblers, and drunkards called themselves in the early years of the 1870s. But when Booth saw his group described as "a volunteer army" in the report proofs, he scratched through the words and wrote "a salvation army" above them. The name stuck, and it has since become a moniker recognized the world round.

The term is particularly fitting. Recognized early on by the militant spirit of its singing, marching, and preaching, the Army is patterned according to military fashion. Its chain of command runs from General (the rank which the international leader carries), down to Colonel, Major, Captain, and Lieutenant. The Chief of Staff oversees the Army's vast territories, four of which are in the United States, their headquarters being New York City, Chicago, Atlanta, and Rancho Palos. Commanders head the territories, and the operations are supervised by commissioned officers, who have successfully completed an intensive two-year cadet training school.

The military model has been particularly effective in helping the Army achieve its goal of preaching the gospel and helping the destitute and poor. It runs dozens of programs designed to do just that, including rehabilitation centers, thrift stores, shelters and low-cost housing, youth programs (Bible School, Boy Scouts and Girl Guards, summer camps, athletic programs), counseling, correctional services, emergency disaster services, and hospital and nursing home visitation. With such programs, the Army has indeed been a salvation to those in need.

Clearinghouses

The employment agencies of the volunteer sector, clearing-houses match volunteers with agencies that need them. They keep track of the volunteer needs of the agencies within their community through updated listings of volunteering opportunities, which they make available to the public through published reports, telephone requests, and personal interviews. A number of clearinghouses also counsel prospective volunteers on how to select voluntary organizations and jobs that best match their own personalities and expectations; some provide administrative assistance to the voluntary agencies themselves.

Four hundred clearinghouses across the country, called Voluntary Action Centers (VAC), are affiliated with VOLUNTEER —The National Center. Local clearinghouses, however, are independently run or are part of larger governmental or voluntary organizations. Since the volunteer needs of clearinghouses are primarily in the areas of administration and counseling, they are looking for people with office, computer, counseling and training skills.

Advocacy Groups

Advocacy groups support their social agendas through public awareness, education, and political lobbying. In some cases advocacy groups either support or administer direct-service programs. Among the more visible of these organizations are the American Association of Retired Persons (AARP), the American Cancer Society, the American Foundation for the Blind, Easter Seals and the National AIDS Network (NAN).

Advocacy groups encompass both national organizations with local branches, such as those listed above, and community-based groups promoting local causes. The volunteer needs of these groups are primarily in the areas of administration, law, public relations, and fundraising.

Direct Service Groups

The most common type of voluntary organizations, direct service groups provide goods and services directly to those in need. Although this group includes large national organizations that offer a variety of services through their local branches, most are community-based organizations. Types of direct service include:

Missions and Shelters: The majority offer temporary shelter, meals, and clothing, although some also provide health care, tutoring, counseling, alcohol rehabilitation, and worship services. The people served include homeless families, adults and children, runaway teens, battered women and severely abused children. Volunteer needs: tutors, counselors, companions and visitors, and recreational leaders.

Soup Kitchens, Food Distributors, Meal Delivery Programs: They are primarily concerned with feeding poor families, the homeless, and the sick that are homebound. Volunteer needs: cooks, servers, clean-up crews, drivers.

Community Centers: They offer a host of programs to meet the needs of their prospective neighborhoods. The range of services provided includes motivational and recreational programs to divert youth from drugs and crime, recreational and support services for the elderly, emergency assistance programs, adult tutoring and pre-school programs. Volunteer needs: tutors, counselors, companions and visitors, and recreational leaders.

Catholic Charities

Catholic Charities was established in 1910 at the Catholic University in Washington, D.C. with the avowed purpose of establishing and furthering the work of charitable organizations, as well as coordinating the social mission of the Catholic Church in the United States.

Through its more than 600 member agencies and institutions, the group provides assistance to the poor through counseling, advocacy, and casework. The Charities' help also extends to the elderly, most of whom are on limited incomes, and to families that are dealing with such problems as strife, drug addiction, and child abuse and neglect. Volunteers are used in most local chapters.

Among the services it offers to families are those for foster care, adoption, maternity, refugee resettlement, shelter, and drug addiction. Catholic Charities also has an extensive program for the elderly, including senior citizen assistance, transportation, home-delivered meals, and employment.

Crisis Intervention Centers, Respite and Support Centers: They offer counseling and emotional support to the disadvantaged, the disabled, or the abused, as well as their families. Some also provide emergency shelter for battered women, abused children, PWAs, runaway and pregnant teens, and alcohol and drug abusers. Many operate telephone hotlines and counseling and support programs for the families of clients. Volunteer needs: supportive people who can provide counseling and comfort to clients and their families, hotline counselors, lawyers and those with medical training.

Halfway Houses and Residential Homes: They provide housing and counseling to the mentally and physically disabled, troubled teens, alcohol and drug abusers, ex-offenders, and pregnant teens. Volunteer needs: people to provide educational and occupational training to residents, counselors, recreational program leaders.

Health Care: Hospitals and clinics, especially those in the inner-city, have been seriously hurt by federal budget cuts. Many are increasing their use of volunteers to help offset their increasing financial deficits. Volunteers are used in children's hospice, physical rehabilitation, and surgical wards to provide comfort and support to patients and their families. Other volunteer needs: admission secretaries, clerical helpers, visitors, staffers of mobile libraries.

Nursing Homes: These for-profit and not-for-profit homes serve as institutions for people, usually the elderly, who need varying degrees of assistance or medical care. Volunteer needs: visitors to talk with or entertain residents, personal care professionals such as barbers or beauticians to provide free or reduced-cost services, people talented in music or arts and crafts to organize recreational programs.

Telephone Hotlines: Telephone counseling centers, or "hotlines," help people deal with any number of traumatic events. They offer direct aid, information, or a listening ear to anyone with access to a phone. The telephones are staffed by volunteers who are trained to listen, counsel, and refer clients to the appropriate place for assistance. Some hotlines offer specialized services, such as programs for rape victims and substance abusers. Others are more general, providing assistance for all types of problems and concerns. Volunteer needs: hotline intake workers, clerical and maintenance workers, fundraisers.

Literacy, Education, and Job Training Centers: These programs emphasize services that help the disadvantaged and dis-

---

Volunteer Entrepreneurs

A recent development in volunteering has been the increase in the number of new programs and organizations that have been created to meet specific needs of the disadvantaged. Though not for everybody, this avenue has been pursued by some ambitious families and individuals across the country. Some of these new projects began small in scope and size and remained so, while others have grown rapidly as people have come to assist the founders in their mission. Examples of this new wave of volunteering include:

New York Cares:
A group of young professional volunteers, New York Cares was founded by Suzette Brooks, a twenty-nine-year-old Harvard Law School graduate. This group, which now has 600 volunteers, works in several New York welfare hotels and homeless shelters; they also do volunteer work with thirty-eight other volunteer organizations on projects such as converting vacant buildings in Brooklyn into homes for the poor. A member's participation in the group ranges from twice a week to once every six months.

John and Mary Barker:
A "two-person mobile shelter," John and Mary Barker twice a week load food, clothing and blankets they have collected from neighbors into the family van. They then go out in search of homeless people who do not go to the missions for help. Their mission of mercy takes them to vacant buildings, alleyways, and train stations in search of the homeless.

Los Angeles Poverty Department (LAPD):
A noted experimental performance artist who has long been concerned about homelessness, John Malped discovered a unique way of using his talents to improve the lives of others. He took a handful of homeless people and trained them to become performance artists in skits he had created about life on skid row. The group, a "movable small theatre," travels around California helping to change the public's view on homelessness and providing the homeless with a support system.

abled improve their situation through employment and education. Some centers teach disadvantaged teens and adults how to read and write, to prepare for high school degree equivalency exams, and to acquire job skills. Many school systems use volunteers to assist teachers in educating their students. Other programs work with the disabled, teaching them occupational and independent living skills. Volunteer needs: teachers and teacher's aids, counselors, physical therapists, administrative assistants.

Multi-Purpose: These direct service organizations offer a number of programs to meet various human-care needs. Multi-service organizations such as The Salvation Army and Catholic Charities offer some or all of the following: shelter and food, maternity care, counseling, job training, health care, substance abuse rehabilitation programs, and services for the elderly and people with disabilities. Volunteer needs: similar to those for single direct service agencies.

Professional Volunteer Associations: Professional organizations, such as a local bar association, an advertising or public relations council, an accountant's association, or a health professional's organization, can offer their services to the needy. This can be done either through offering to help the human-care agency itself or by setting up a direct service program. Volunteer needs: professionals from all fields.

CORPORATE, SCHOOL and CHURCH VOLUNTEER PROGRAMS

Some potential volunteers may be attracted to volunteer programs that are administered through organizations they are affiliated with. For instance, there are over 1,200 corporations nationwide that sponsor employee volunteer programs. Continental Bank, for one, has adopted an inner-city high school and nine nearby elementary schools. The bank's employees volunteer to tutor, act as mentors, and provide career guidance to the schools' students. Time, Inc.'s employees serve as literacy tutors in fifteen cities. The employees in the District of Columbia's Department of Transportation offer tutorial services to an inner-city high school and provide volunteer support to a senior citizen's center and a homeless shelter.

While most employees do their volunteer work on their own time, more and more corporations, such as IBM, General Motors, and McDonalds, have developed "Loaned Executive Programs." In these programs, an employee can work full-time at a non-profit organization for a specified period. During the "loan" period, the employee's salary and benefits are paid by the corporation. IBM's loan program is one of the nation's oldest. Since 1971, IBM employees have provided full-time management, computer and financial planning assistance to organizations such as the American Red Cross, the National Urban League, and the National

What Can I Do?

There is a volunteer job out there that matches your interests and talents. Ask yourself the questions pertinent to your situation. Are you a(n):

Aspiring Actor? Singer? Perform in musical or theatrical benefits for the needy.

Athletic Enthusiast? Get involved in the Special Olympics. Devote your marathon participation to those that promote causes you believe in, or help sponsor a new marathon, cyclathon, or whatever-athon.

Artist? Teach art at a community center for disadvantaged kids or in recreational centers for the elderly or people with handicaps. Help paint a mission or shelter.

Avid Reader? Record books onto tapes for the blind; read books to the elderly in nursing homes, or teach illiterate youths and adults how to read.

Computer Genius? Assist clearinghouses, advocacy organizations and other agencies in using the power of computers to effectively accomplish their goals.

Design Student? Adapt clothing to meet special needs of people with disabilities. Propose architectural changes to promote accessibility, helping people with disabilities to be more comfortable and self-sufficient at home, in the workplace, and in public.

Doctor? Work at a local hospital or at a not-for-profit clinic providing medical care or assisting the medical staff with patient care, family support programs, or administration.

Good Listener? Work on a crisis hotline for teenagers, battered women or abused children. Be a counselor for families of the disabled or People With AIDS.

Commission for the Prevention of Child Abuse.

Unions and fraternal and membership organizations also provide their members with opportunities to become volunteers. Union locals in Dayton, Sacramento, Philadelphia, Washington, D.C. and many other cities have contributed their skills to renovate homeless shelters, fix toys for children with disabilities, and upgrade child care centers. Other organizations, such as the Lions Club International, the Knights of Columbus, the National Council of Jewish Woman, the Association of Junior Leagues, the Urban League, and most college fraternities and sororities, also sponsor service projects in which their members can get involved.

What Can I Do?—Continued

Gourmet Cook? Prepare meals at a mission or food bank for the homeless or the disadvantaged. Give cooking lessons at a living skills center for the disabled.

Lawyer? Become an advocate. Lobby legislators and the public for the changes to improve the plight of the homeless, the poor, people with disabilities, or any social group.

Mountain Man or Woman? Go along on camping trips with disabled or disadvantaged youths. Become a Scoutmaster for the Boy Scouts or Girl Scouts.

Mr. Fixit? Assist your local voluntary agencies in maintaining their facilities. Join a program rehabilitating homes for the poor and homeless.

Night Owl? Work the overnight shift once a month at a shelter for the homeless, runaway teens or abused families.

Olympic Swimmer? Work as a swimming pool therapist with physically disabled youths learning to use and strengthen their muscles.

Private Eye Hopeful? Hunt for manufacturers or businesses with surpluses in food, clothing, or other goods, and match them up with an organization that can get them to those in need.

Race Car Driver? Deliver meals to the homebound elderly. Provide transportation for people with disabilities to get to therapy and recreational activities.

Talkative? Join a public speaking group for a cause you believe in. Give lectures to promote public awareness, involvement, or donations.

Colleges offer students many opportunities to become involved in volunteer projects. One of the largest student programs, The University of Illinois Volunteer Illini, enlists the help of more than 1,000 students in various volunteer projects. Nationwide, well over five hundred colleges and universities have active student volunteer programs.

High school students can also get involved. Suitland High School in Maryland, which has one of the top volunteer programs in the country, is a good example. Winner of the Presidential Volunteer Action Award, Suitland students provide peer counseling to students with academic or personal problems; they also perform volunteer work at a local nursing home and at a center for people with disabilities.

Religious institutions offer even more opportunities for the volunteer. Volunteers are needed to assist in the running of the church, from teaching Sunday school, to ushering, to doing office work. In addition, volunteers can also get involved in the church's outreach programs, which offer assistance to the homeless, the destitute, or other disadvantaged people in the neighborhood. One of the most successful church outreach programs is the Interfaith Hospitality Network for the Homeless in New Jersey. Through its 15,000 volunteers, the churches in the Network provide food, shelter and clothing to thousands of homeless people. Two Chicago Churches, Fourth Presbyterian and LaSalle Street Church, enlist their members to serve as volunteer tutors and mentors to at-risk teens from a nearby housing project.

From churches to corporations, organizations provide the potential volunteer with numerous additional opportunities to help others. They also provide an added volunteer benefit—the ability to work together with friends and co-workers. So before you sign up with another organization, check to see if your employer, church, fraternal or business organization sponsors a volunteer program that would be of interest to you.

BOARD and COMMITTEE POSITIONS

In addition to the volunteer needs listed under direct service organizations, there is also a need for people to serve on the boards and committees of volunteer agencies. Volunteers who sit on these boards and committees set the organization's policies, direction, and operational plans. The committee members also provide leadership to the staff and monitor the organization's progress. Depending on its size and complexity, the agency may have volunteer needs for one or more of the following committees:

Executive Committee: Often made up of members of the agency's Board of Trustees, the executive committee attempts to make the Board's job easier by narrowing in and reporting on the most important projects. In doing so, they help define and direct an agency's mission.

Finance Committee: This committee keeps an agency fiscally responsible, making sure it operates within its budget, reviewing the availability of funds for new initiatives, meeting present financial obligations and regularly reporting on the budget.

Planning Committee: Most of the energies of the committee are spent developing plans to realize the goals of the agency and the Board of Trustees. This includes defining long-term objectives, creating operating budgets, and setting up special committees.

Public Relations Committee: The committee keeps the public informed of the agency's projects through news releases, press conferences, and advertisements. Their efforts are used to gain public support within a community, to lobby governmental bodies on behalf of their agencies' clients, to advertise services the agency provides, to recruit volunteers, and to raise money during funding campaigns.

Special Projects Committee: Also known as "ad-hoc" committees, these groups are formed to handle a specific project. Such committees have been called to determine the real need of certain programs or to devise an advocacy campaign to get lawmakers to support their cause.

VOLUNTEER POLICY

Another difference between human-care organizations is the philosophy and operating policy behind their volunteer programs. This affects each agency's need for volunteers, its training program, and volunteer rights and responsibilities. Ultimately, these factors impact how well you will perform and enjoy your volunteer work.

Training

Some volunteer programs run regularly scheduled training programs for prospective volunteers. The training normally explains the agency's mission and operating procedures and teaches volunteers the skills and techniques they will need to per-

United Way of America

Because of its very successful Crusade of Mercy fundraising campaign, the United Way is probably the most widely recognized nonprofit organization in America. Founded in Denver in 1887, the United Way has provided funding and support for thousands of social service organizations across the country for over one hundred years.

In Chicago alone, the United Way raised and allocated over fifty million dollars for 380 local social service and community organizations in 1988. These organizations supported by the United Way of Chicago embrace a broad spectrum of community needs: health care, housing, job training, programs for the elderly and assistance for people with disabilities. Other social problems addressed by these organizations include hunger, domestic violence, child abuse, teen pregnancy, illiteracy, AIDS and juvenile delinquency.

In addition to allocating funds to social care organizations, the United Way provides administrative support and offers training programs to help these agencies run more efficiently. Through their volunteer centers, the United Way recruits and refers volunteers to organizations that need them.

The driving force behind the success of the United Way is its volunteer corps, numbering in the tens of thousands. From board members to clerical workers, these volunteers manage the crucial task of fundraising and the fund distribution and allocation process. They, along with the paid staff, make the United Way the outstanding umbrella organization it is today. And because of its efforts, thousands of social organizations across the country are better able to meet the needs of their communities.

form their jobs. The programs usually extend over a number of sessions and may be more or less extensive depending on the nature of the work involved. Crisis counselors and literacy tutors, for example, are given intensive training, while clerical workers are given less.

Smaller organizations however, may provide on-the-job training. The volunteer in this case will be expected to learn the functions of his or her job by working with experienced volunteers or staff members. This method of training works best when the job functions are relatively straightforward or when the volunteer has previous related experience.

Volunteer Management

While some organizations have a full-time volunteer supervisor on staff, many use their executive director or other per-

Disaster Volunteers: The Red Cross

When former victims of fires, earthquakes, floods or other natural disasters think of volunteers, they most likely think of the disaster volunteers of the American Red Cross. Within hours of an emergency, Red Cross's disaster volunteers are there, providing clothing, shelter, and food to the disaster's victims.

Unlike other volunteering assignments, disaster volunteers don't have regularly scheduled hours or a day of the week when they perform their volunteer assignment. To the contrary, disaster volunteers are always on call, prepared to assist whenever an unfortunate disaster occurs.

Of course, the American Red Cross has other types of volunteer assignments as well. Volunteers can work with the Red Cross blood bank, its overseas military personnel support programs, its health and safety training programs, and with Red Cross programs to help seniors and people with Aids. But it is the work of the disaster volunteers that many find most fulfilling.

People of all skill levels and ages are needed to become disaster volunteers. All that is required is good health and a desire to help. So if you are looking for a challenging volunteer assignment, give your local Red Cross office a call.

sonnel to manage their volunteers. In most cases, a full-time volunteer supervisor will be able to give the volunteers more attention and direction. A supervisor can conduct volunteer performance reviews more often, offer ongoing training sessions, and provide social and recognition events for volunteers on a regular basis.

At agencies where the executive director or other staff person supervises volunteers on a part-time basis, he or she will not have the time to pamper volunteers like the full-time supervisor can. In this case, it is important for the volunteers to be proactive in seeking feedback on their work or asking for additional training when they feel it's needed.

THE ORGANIZATION and YOU

A voluntary organization, like any business or corporation, has its own environment and structure, a way of doing business that has been developed over the years. Its climate will greatly affect your volunteer work there, so look closely at each organization—at its structure, operating philosophy, the way it delivers its services—and consider how its personality matches your own.

CHAPTER FOUR

Finding the Right Volunteer Job

WITH THIRTEEN years of experience in social service and volunteer management behind him, James Lindsay speaks with the insight and authority that comes with a thorough understanding of one's field. So when asked how a person can become an effective volunteer, he went right to the heart of the matter: "One of the most important factors in being successful in volunteering is getting placed in an organization which is doing the kind of volunteer work that is right for you."

Having placed over 6,000 volunteers with local organizations in his seven years as executive director of The Volunteer Clearinghouse of Washington, D.C., Lindsay and his staff have become adept at getting volunteers into the jobs that best suit them. "At the clearinghouse we try to find out what the prospective volunteers are interested in and match them with a volunteer job that meets those interests," he says. "Otherwise, many of them drop out, at least temporarily, because they don't enjoy the work or find it challenging enough."

Like most directors, Lindsay has found that when volunteers are working in jobs that best suit them, they are far more effective. Volunteers who enjoy and feel comfortable in their work are better able not only to help others, but also to make a stronger contribution in helping a human care agency deliver its services and run more efficiently.

Only you can determine which volunteer position is right for you. As in choosing any job, you have a lot of freedom: you choose your area of service, your time commitment, the organization you want to volunteer through, and in many cases, the job you want to do. But use that freedom wisely, keeping in mind what you know about yourself, in order to maximize your volunteer experience.

Getting any volunteer job is easy; a first interview will often get you hired. Landing the *right* volunteer job demands some effort. It requires that you take the time to consider some basic questions: What are your reasons for volunteering? What benefits do you want to gain? What tasks do you most enjoy doing? Do you have any special skills and talents that you would like to put to use? This chapter will lead you through a step-by-step process to help you answer these questions and find the volunteer organization that will best make use of your unique talents and interests.

The Good Heart Book's recommended procedure for choosing a volunteering position is broken down into eight steps:

1. Make a list of your reasons for wanting to volunteer and the benefits you expect to receive from your volunteer service.

TIPS FROM VOLUNTEERS
How to Choose the Right Volunteer Job

Mary Lu: "The important thing is to pursue your interest honestly and vigorously. Whatever it is that you truly enjoy, whether it's singing, cooking, flying kites, or fixing cars, chances are that you can find a way to make your interest benefit someone else."

John: "To get started, pick out an area that you are concerned about or interested in, and force yourself to do something, no matter how small. Once you get started, it's habit-forming."

Rose: "If you don't know what to do, the best place to start is with old people or small kids. The old people have been forgotten, with no one to care for them. The real small kids, they're reaching out for somebody to care."

Carolyn: "Go to a shelter and hang out with the kids for a while. Once you go, you're hooked."

Laura: "For a year I thought about volunteering; I almost signed up twice. But once I heard about being a literacy tutor, I decided that was right for me and signed up. I think what's most important is finding the right job."

2. Analyze your time schedule to determine how much time you are willing and able to devote to volunteering.

3. Select a social problem area you want to work in.

4. Contact a volunteer clearinghouse or bureau for information on available volunteering jobs in your chosen area.

5. Determine which of these organizations is best for you.

6. Determine which volunteer job will best utilize your skills and meet your volunteering expectations.

7. Contact your chosen volunteer organizations for an interview.

8. Prepare yourself to get off to a good start in your new volunteering assignment.

Some of you may have your own method of deciding how to get involved as a volunteer. Nevertheless, read through the steps to make sure you don't overlook any important factors. There is a checklist at the end of this chapter to help you organize your thoughts.

STEP 1: MOTIVATIONS AND EXPECTATIONS

The first step in the decision-making process is to make a list of your reasons for becoming a volunteer. Consult the volunteering benefits and motivations section in chapter 2. Be as specific as possible when compiling your list. Most volunteers want to make a positive difference in the lives of others. However, while one volunteer may be motivated to push for social changes to find a longer-term solution, another may be motivated to help solve the immediate crisis. While the first volunteer may be better suited for advocacy work, the latter might be happier in a direct service job, such as in a soup kitchen or shelter.

Helping others is only one of the reasons people look to become volunteers. Some people may be looking to do something meaningful with their lives; others might be primarily interested in learning new skills. For a volunteer's experience to be fulfilling and meaningful, his or her expectations must be met to a certain degree.

Mark, a Chicago dockworker, was concerned about homelessness and wanted to do something about it. He was also interested in learning more about construction. Habitat for Humanity was the perfect organization for him. "I joined Habitat for Humanity," he says, "because I could learn carpentry and drywalling while building homes for the homeless." Mark says he enjoys his volunteer work—not only is he satisfying his desire to help the homeless, but he is developing skills he has wanted to acquire for some time.

Caroline, a counselor, also had specific reasons for volunteering. Recently transferred to Boston, she thought joining a volunteer organization would be a good way to make new friends and get to know the city. "I joined a women's shelter in Cambridge," she says, "where I met some wonderful people who have been extremely helpful to me in adjusting to life in a new city."

Like Mark and Caroline, you also need to know what you expect from volunteering. Once you know what you want, you can better choose an agency that helps you get it. But before you move on to that decision, you need to consider how you are going to find the time for your new volunteering commitment.

STEP 2: FINDING THE TIME

For most of us, time is a precious commodity. Meeting all of our obligations to our careers, families, friends, and social activities leaves us little time for ourselves, let alone time to help others. As busy as we are, however, we must find time to take care of ourselves. Making time for activities that contribute to our physical and spiritual health, such as exercise and reflection, is essential if we want to lead a contented and fulfilling life. In fact, we all should examine our busy schedules from time to time and ask ourselves the question in the slogan of Apple Computer's volunteer program: "Your life is busy—but is it full?"

Volunteering is one way of filling out your life. Helping others allows you to meet many of your own emotional and spiritual needs. Volunteering should not be viewed as a minor activity you do when you can find the time, but as an important part of your lifestyle. Volunteering should be given priority, even when it means curtailing the amount of time you spend doing other activities.

For John, who is single and socially active, volunteering

means giving up one night a week with his friends. "Sometimes I miss out on something, but for all I get from volunteering, it's worth it." Ann also admits that her volunteering work with the elderly requires some sacrifice. "Some weeks I don't feel like going simply because I have so much to do. But once I'm there, I'm always glad I made the commitment."

Making a Time Schedule

To determine how you can realistically incorporate volunteering into your routine, prepare a time schedule. Make a list of your daily activities, including such necessities as grocery shopping, visiting friends, doing laundry, as well as leisure activities and down time for yourself. Look to see if you have free time or activities you could spend less time doing. Your analysis will tell you how much time you can realistically commit to volunteering and which days of the week would be most convenient for it.

Later when you contact a clearinghouse for information, you will find out the minimum time requirements and preferred working hours for various volunteer organizations. Most organizations require a volunteer to commit to working with them for a certain amount of time, with a specified number of service

Finding the Time, Making the Difference

David, an attorney, admits that he doesn't "have the time" for the volunteer work he does for Habitat for Humanity. "I'm just overloaded at work, and I work fairly long hours, often on weekends." His wife is also an attorney who is just as busy, and they have a four-month-old baby. So it is no understatement when he says, "Time is precious to me." It doesn't help that Habitat's work is done on Saturdays, the day David most wants to spend with his growing family. As he sees it, there are no easy answers. "It's a real tough conflict, and things get displaced. It can be as trivial as not getting your shirts to the cleaner and not having clean shirts for the following week. Not running all the errands you have to run on Saturday, or hopping a cab after work to sit through several hours of a meeting on organizing what to do next on the project." But even with the pressures on his time, David is "always glad" when he has gone and worked at the site. "The work is very gratifying when you're there."

hours per month. The total time commitment can range anywhere from three months to a year, and the required hours per month can be as few as eight or as many as twenty. Knowing your time availability will help you eliminate organizations whose time requirements are too much for you.

For those of you with busy home or work lives, there are programs which have flexible time requirements. Some agencies allow volunteers to do clerical work and fundraising from their homes. For the busy executive, there are companies with volunteer programs that loan their paid workers to volunteer agencies during working hours. Check with your company's personnel department to see if your employer has a volunteer loan program.

In analyzing your availability, carefully weigh the balance between being generous with your time and over-committing yourself. Overextending yourself leads to stress and frustration, so start slowly. You can always make a greater time commitment later if you find you are able.

STEP 3: WHO TO HELP

For some of you, determining which social area to volunteer in is relatively easy. You may have had some previous volunteer experience or long had an interest in certain social issues. Perhaps a college class, a book, a documentary, or a news feature caught your interest and made you aware of the seriousness of a problem. Or maybe you have known someone who was living in some type of crisis situation. And now as you make a decision to volunteer, you already know what area you want to look into. This was true of Caroline. Her involvement in a women's shelter came about in part because of her education at a women's college which strongly emphasized working on feminist issues outside of the classroom. Violence against women disturbed her enough so that she knew she "wanted to get involved in eradicating it" and signed up at the shelter.

But there are many of you who are undecided about who to help. While concerned about the problems of our society, you may not feel more passionately about one issue than another. To get an idea of the range of major social problems in which volunteers commonly become involved, read through the chapters in Part II of this book. See which of the issues moves your

A Personal Inventory

Ask yourself these questions before you choose a volunteering job:

Time:
- How much free time do I have available to work?
- How many hours a week would I like to volunteer?
- How much of a commitment am I willing to make? How many months am I able to commit to a volunteer job?

Skills/Interests/Experience:
- Why do I want to be a volunteer? Will the job I choose fulfill those motivations?
- Have I done volunteer work before? What did I like/dislike about it? Do I want to do something similar again? Something different?
- Do I have any interests or hobbies that I would like to use in my volunteer job?
- Do I have any skills from my career that I would like to apply to a volunteer job?

Setting:
- Do I have a geographic preference? How far am I willing to travel to do volunteer work?
- What kind of atmosphere would I like to work in? Quiet?
- Fast-paced?
- Do I want to work inside or outside?
- What kind of place do I want to work in? Hospital?
- School? Nursing Home? Office? Shelter? Soup Kitchen?
- Do I want to work independently or with other volunteers or staff?

Clientele:
- What age group do I want to work with? Infants? Children?
- Teenagers? Adults? Elderly?
- Do I want to work with people who have disabilities? What kind of disabilities? Physical? Mental? Emotional? All?
- Do I want to work one-on-one with a person or with a group of people?

Source, brochure, United Way of Massachusetts Bay, Voluntary Action Center. Used with permission.

social conscience. Also, read through the following list to see if any of the circumstances listed applies to you. It was prepared to help stimulate your thoughts about social areas you might naturally be drawn to, be best suited for, or most enjoy working in.

Past Personal Experience

At one time you may have experienced the hardships endured by the needy profiled in this book. You may have been poor, hungry, or abused as a child; you may have had problems with drugs or alcohol or run away from home as a teenager. If this is true for you, consider helping others who are going through a similar problem. Your past may serve as a means of breaking down the barriers separating you and the needy, and allow you to help them.

Those You Know

Look around you. Chances are you know someone, or know of someone, who needs help. Perhaps a family member, friend, or distant acquaintance attempted suicide, is functionally illiterate, or has a physical handicap. Now that you have been exposed to the problem on a personal level, consider helping others overcome it. In some cases, a family member or friend can be directly helped by your volunteering efforts.

Your Background

Think about issues facing those of your own age, gender, race, or ethnicity. Women may want to help battered wives or rape victims. Black Americans might be drawn to the plight of inner-city families living in poverty. Ethnic and minority groups may have a particular interest in promoting literacy and education causes, while members of the gay and lesbian community might want to assist in AIDS prevention programs. Teenagers might consider volunteering at a local teen hotline, while the elderly may want to visit nursing homes or older shut-ins.

Your Occupation And Skills

You can use your special talents or the knowledge gained from your occupation for the benefit of others. Educators may want to teach illiterate adults, while a nurse or doctor may choose working with inner-city hospitals or not-for-profit clinics. For many prospective volunteers, finding a social problem area in which they are uniquely qualified to serve is the easiest, most efficient way to begin volunteering.

Adopt A Cause

After reading through the various social problems covered in Part II of this book and considering your past experiences and background, you have probably found a social problem that concerns you. As Mary Lu, an economist, puts it, "Volunteering isn't going out and volunteering someplace; it's getting involved in something you believe in." Find the problem area that generates the greatest concern in you and make that cause your own!

STEP 4: USING VOLUNTEER CLEARINGHOUSES

Now that you know the benefits you expect to receive from volunteering and the social problem area you want to work in, you can move on to Step Four: contacting your local volunteer clearinghouse. There you can begin the process of collecting information about volunteer organizations that provide services within the social problem area you have chosen.

Using volunteering clearinghouses or bureaus is the most efficient way of finding out what volunteering opportunities are available. The "employment agencies" of volunteering, clearinghouses match volunteers with organizations that need them. They can provide you with a list of jobs available in your chosen area of service. The clearinghouse can also give you important background information on the volunteer organizations you are interested in, such as the kind of volunteers they are looking for, time commitments, working conditions, and the type of training offered.

Most clearinghouses require prospective volunteers to discuss their volunteering plans with a counselor. With some clearinghouses, this "interview" can be done over the phone, while others prefer that you come into their offices. During the interview, the counselor will find out your reasons for volunteering, the area of service you are interested in, and the job in which you would like to be placed. "We have a database of current volunteer needs that are categorized on computer by skills and area of service," says Christine Franklin, former Vice President of the Massachusetts Bay United Way. "Based on the interview, the counselor will provide the prospective volunteer with several opportunities the counselor feels are appropriate for both the applicant and the agency seeking volunteers."

Clearinghouse counselors are experienced in social service and volunteering, and Franklin encourages prospective volunteers to use them. "Many times volunteers are unrealistic about what they want to accomplish or what they expect from volunteering," she says. "The counselors can be a great help in pointing out volunteering concerns or questions you might have overlooked."

Using a clearinghouse to find out the current volunteer needs of organizations in your area can save you a lot of time and frustration in your search. For some volunteer jobs in social problem areas that are considered "fashionable," the supply of volunteers may exceed the number of jobs available. This is often the case for public relations, tutoring, and fundraising positions. It can be difficult to get volunteer jobs in current high-profile social problem areas such as AIDS, homelessness, and illiteracy within the San Francisco area. A call to a clearinghouse can quickly tell you which jobs are available and which are not.

Volunteer clearinghouses are located in cities and counties across the country. One national network of 400 clearinghouses called Voluntary Action Centers, is affiliated with VOLUNTEER —The National Center. Many areas also have local clearinghouses that are run by government, private or religious organizations. In addition, some advocacy groups serve as clearinghouses for their particular social problem area, such as illiteracy or child abuse. A list of clearinghouses you can contact is provided in the directory section of this book; additional clearinghouses can be found in your local phone book.

Although they offer prospective volunteers a wide variety of services, clearinghouses cannot by themselves find you the right job. They are only a resource. As an applicant, you are still responsible for determining which organization and volunteer job is best for you. When you know what you want to accomplish in volunteering then call a counselor. It is only then that they can most effectively help you find the volunteering position that is right for you.

STEPS 5 AND 6: SELECTING THE RIGHT VOLUNTARY ORGANIZATION AND JOB

After your meeting with a clearinghouse counselor, you should have enough information to decide what organization to join and what type of work to do. Review chapter 3, Human Care Organizations, as well as the information you have received from the clearinghouse about available volunteering opportunities. Then read through the following sections, Steps 5 and 6, before making your decision.

STEP 5: VOLUNTARY ORGANIZATIONS

In chapter 3, the differences among volunteer organizations were discussed. Some organizations are small and informal, and consequently may be more flexible with working hours, work assignments and time commitments. Larger organizations, with multiple administrative levels and stricter operating procedures, may be more stringent. With larger operating budgets, they can offer such benefits as formal classroom training, large supervisory staffs, and a prestigious reference on your resume.

The working environment or *culture* differs from one agency to the next. While one person may feel comfortable working in a structured, fast-paced environment, such as is found in large corporations, another person may prefer a small office environment. You must consider your own personality when deciding on the type of organizational structure that is best for you.

Prospective volunteers should also know what an organization expects and requires of them. Most have minimum time commitments, as well as training and orientation programs that volunteers are required to attend. While training programs in some organizations are short, in others they are more extensive. Many hotline counseling jobs, for example, require forty hours or more of training, some of which is spread out over a number of weekends.

Read the mission statements and operating philosophies of the organizations you are interested in. Talk to people who have volunteered there. Then decide whether their requirements, structures, and atmosphere are right for you.

STEP 6: VOLUNTEER JOBS

Since volunteer jobs are based on the particular needs of the organization, you may need to be flexible in selecting one. A homeless mission may have a great need for food preparers and servers but have only a few positions for office workers. The

What Volunteers Do

Below are the answers given to the question "In which of these areas have you done some volunteer work in the past month?" The top fifteen jobs are listed in descending order, from most to least mentioned.

Aide/Assistant to paid employee	7.6%
Assisting elderly or handicapped	7.3%
Aide to clergy	7.1%
Driver	4.3%
Committee member	3.6%
Baby-sitter	3.3%
Youth group leader or aide	3.1%
Parish visitor or missionary	3.1%
Office work	2.8%
Teacher or tutor	2.6%
Choir member	2.3%
Cleaning or janitorial work	2.2%
Coach or recreational volunteer	2.1%
Sunday school or bible teacher	2.1%
Board Member or trustee	1.6%

From *Giving and Volunteering in the United States*, a survey conducted by The Gallup Organization for INDEPENDENT SECTOR, 1990.

needs of an organization which matches volunteers with dis-advantaged children, such as Big Brothers and Big Sisters, is lim-ited to the number of children who join the program. Think of several jobs you would enjoy doing as a volunteer. Flexibility will help alleviate some of the frustration in your job search.

The first step in selecting a volunteering job is to determine what skills or talents you may want to utilize. While some people may want to do work that is similar to their occupation, others may want to do something completely different. Think about hobbies, job skills, or other interests you may have. Then decide which of them you would like to use in your volunteer work.

While considering job opportunities, make sure you are qual-ified for the volunteering assignment you want. If you don't have the personality or training to do a certain job in the paid work-place, don't expect a volunteer organization to allow you to "experiment" on them. Today, more and more professionals are becoming volunteers, and organizations are finding it easier to fill their highly skilled positions with people trained in those fields. You can expect to get a position in which you can grow and learn new skills, but be realistic.

It is also important that you understand the types of personal commitments required of volunteers. Direct service work brings you into contact with people in need, but one-on-one volunteer-ing requires a real commitment to another person. Being a Big Brother, a Foster Grandparent, or a regular visitor to a particular elderly or disabled person requires developing a personal relationship. Make sure you are willing and able to commit to that relationship before you begin it.

As you select a volunteer job, you must face certain realities about volunteer work: it can be difficult. Hospitals, nursing homes, and missions are not always easy places to work. Helping people with AIDS, disabilities, or emotional problems can be ex-tremely taxing. You will receive many personal rewards by helping people in these difficult circumstances, but don't over-do it. If you know that you feel uncomfortable being around sick people, don't volunteer to work in a hospital. To find out what working conditions are appropriate for you, consider the following questions:

• How would you feel about coming into direct contact with a homeless person, an elderly person, an abused child, a sick person? How would you feel about physically touching them?

- How would you feel about working in unfamiliar neighborhoods?
- How would you feel about working in settings such as missions, hospitals, or nursing homes?
- How would you feel about performing direct service tasks, such as serving meals, manning a telephone hotline, tutoring, or transporting people with disabilities?
- Is it important that you do certain types of work, such as public relations or clerical work, or are you willing to do whatever job the volunteer organization needs to have done?
- How personal do you want to get? Do you want your volunteer work to enter into your private life?

The point is to visualize yourself in a particular volunteer situation. Try to ask yourself specific questions like the ones above. This will give you a good idea of what you really want and do not want from your volunteering, and it will help you in selecting a volunteer job that is most compatible with your needs.

After you have answered the above questions, you can narrow down your list to a few organizations that have jobs that suit you. Make sure that any selection you make at this point is consistent with the list of benefits you are looking to gain from volunteering. For instance, if you are looking to learn new skills, make sure the organization you select has a training program or a job that allows you to develop new abilities. If you want to meet new people, select a job that will allow you to work with other volunteers. If you are motivated to volunteer by a desire to accomplish something meaningful, you should consider an organization with clearly defined goals so you can get feedback on the results of your efforts.

After determining what type of job you would most like to do, review the clearinghouse list for similar openings in your chosen area of service. If you find that the job you wanted is not available, look to see if a similar one is available in another social problem area. However, if one of your primary reasons for volunteering is to help alleviate a particular social problem, you may want to temporarily accept any job opening in that area. Find an organization that is flexible and understanding, and explain to

How Deeply Involved Do I Want to Become?

In choosing a direct service volunteer job, one question prospective volunteers have to ask themselves is: How personally involved do I want to become? Of course, in any volunteer assignment, some personal involvement with those you want to help is necessary. In fact, many program administrators believe that some personal involvement is crucial to becoming an effective volunteer. Lynda Williams, an administrator for Family Friends says, "You are not effective in other people's lives unless you get personally involved."

But volunteers differ on the extent to which they want to become personally involved with the disadvantaged. Some volunteers prefer to keep their distance, while others might go as far to invite the people they help into their home. Whatever the case, volunteers should understand that the job they choose is the primary factor in determining the level of personal involvement required.

One-to-one volunteering jobs, such as being a Big Brother or sponsoring an elderly person, will naturally require a high degree of personal contact and involvement. Ann, who visits an elderly woman each week, has become very involved with her elderly friend. Ann helps her write letters, takes her shopping and to the hospital, and has even met many of her family members. Laura, a literacy tutor, helped her homeless student find an apartment. Debbie, a Big Sister, gets involved in all facets of her "little sister's" life, including her schoolwork and family problems.

A volunteer's level of personal involvement is lessened when he or she works with groups of people. A volunteer coach's time and energy would be divided among a number of children, greatly limiting the opportunities to develop close, personal relationships with each child. A volunteer who wants to minimize personal involvement should choose fundraising or advocacy work.

To be happy in your volunteer work, give serious thought to how deeply involved you want to become with another person. Do not sign up to be a Big Brother if you are not fully prepared to bring a new person into your life. You would probably be happier working with a group. If you are unsure as to the level of personal commitment required in a particular volunteer assignment, ask your clearinghouse counselor or the agency's interviewer.

the organization administrator what work you would prefer doing. Consider staying with the organization if the administrator commits to offering you a job similar to the one you want when it becomes available.

STEP 7: YOUR INTERVIEW

Once you have selected an organization, set up an interview with its director of volunteers. Before you go, find out what type of interview it will be. If you are applying for an unskilled position and many of them are open, the interviewer may be interested in convincing you that you would fit into his or her organization. However, if you are applying for a skilled position or to an organization that has a surplus of volunteers, you will have to convince the interviewer that you are the right person for the job. As in business, every person that applies is not accepted by the volunteer organization or offered the particular job he or she desires. Contact your local clearinghouse for information about what to expect from the interview.

Most agencies will attempt to place you in a position that will meet your needs and expectations. With many organizations, however, the work you are given will to a large extent be determined by their specific needs. If the job is not at all what you had expected or wanted, try the next organization on your list. Finding the best volunteer job for you is a lot like finding the right career—it may take a while. But when you do, you can look forward to a long period of satisfying work.

STEP 8: GETTING OFF TO A GOOD START

With your decision made, you are anxious to get in there and start making a difference! That's great, but be sure to take some time to learn about the organization and its operating procedures. Get to know your fellow workers, especially the organization's administrators and your direct supervisors. Find out how they view the organization, its mission, and the role of volunteers.

During your interview, you learned as much as you could about the organization. But you can only learn so much in an hour. Now is the time to find out how the organization really works. Ask questions and read their procedure manual if there is one. Time spent learning about your new environment now can save you time and energy later on.

The organization should have some type of orientation program for new volunteers. This usually includes an introduction to the paid staff and an explanation of the basic operating procedures. Use this period to your advantage. Get to know the paid staffers. Their experience and insight in the social services could prove invaluable to you as you learn your volunteering job.

Spend time talking to your direct supervisor. You probably interviewed with an administrator, with whom you discussed your expectations and job description. If your supervisor is different from your interviewer, do not assume that he or she knows what you discussed in that interview. Find out directly what your supervisor expects from you, and make sure that he or she knows what your own expectations are.

Finally, do not take the upcoming orientation and training programs for granted. They are opportunities for you to learn how to effectively help the people served by the agency. Volunteering is serious business. The welfare of people in need depends on how well you and others do your jobs. Read chapter 5 on how to maximize your opportunity to help others. And give your best!

Volunteering Checklist

1. Have you made a list of your reasons for volunteering and the benefits you want to get from it?

2. Have you determined how much time you can realistically commit to volunteering? Have you made a time schedule to see how volunteering can fit into your life?

3. Have you determined which area of social concern you want to work in?

4. Have you contacted a local clearinghouse or other source for information about available volunteering opportunities?

5. Have you determined which volunteer organizations might be best for you?

6. Have you determined which available jobs you would like to do?

7. Have you visited your chosen organization for an interview?

8.   Now that you have made your choice, are you clear on what the organization expects from you? Is your supervisor aware of what you expect from your volunteer experience?

CHAPTER FIVE

Growing As An Effective Volunteer

NOW THAT YOU have found the volunteer job that best fits you, you can begin channeling your energies and enthusiasm toward helping others in need. But as you begin your work, be aware that enthusiasm alone is not enough to make you an effective volunteer. Volunteering is a learning, growing process, and as with most jobs, you will become better at it as you gain insight and experience. Over time you will learn how to recognize the needs of those you are helping and how to best get them the types of services they require. Most importantly, you will learn how to motivate and inspire them to improve their lives. In short, you will learn how to become a knowledgeable, effective volunteer.

Completing her first full year as a hotline counselor for the Metrohelp-National Runaway switchboard, Ellen has grown through both her own efforts and her volunteering experience into an effective crisis counselor. "At first," says Ellen, "I was apprehensive about my abilities to help people in a crisis situation. The kids that called had such serious problems: drugs, sexual abuse, suicide, and whatever else." Ellen's apprehension lead her to add to her forty hours of volunteer training by reading books on counseling and teen problems and by seeking additional information from professionals in the field.

With a year of experience, training, and outside research behind her, Ellen has become a confident and effective crisis counselor. Like many volunteers who are truly committed to helping others in the best way they can, she knows that the better she is, the greater the impact she will have on her callers.

This chapter will guide you through five steps which will help you become a better, more effective volunteer in your area of service:

1. Learning more about the specific volunteer task you have chosen.
2. Learning more about the social problem area you are involved in.
3. Learning how to listen to, motivate, and encourage people in need.
4. Learning to advocate for the disadvantaged.
5. Learning to encourage others to volunteer.

LEARNING YOUR VOLUNTEERING JOB

As a new volunteer, you will be required to attend a training and orientation program run by the agency you have signed up with. Through lectures, discussions with experienced volunteers, and practice sessions, the training program will attempt to prepare you for your volunteer assignment. But even the best training cannot completely prepare you to handle the many facets of your job. Many volunteers admit to still feeling unprepared after having completed their training. Many have lingering questions about their responsibilities, the availability of other social services, and just how to best counsel the people they have volunteered to help.

Volunteer Training

All voluntary agencies provide some sort of training for new volunteers. While the extent of training is determined by job requirements and agency policies, all volunteers should be familiar with the following items after training:

- A general understanding of the agency's mission, client policies and services.
- The agency's volunteer policy, including dress code, conduct, attendance, and performance measurement.
- A general understanding of the nature and the problems of the agency's clients.
- Who your direct supervisor is and what responsibilities he or she has concerning your development as a volunteer.
- How you should interact with the agency's clients.
- What the procedures are for getting needed services for the agency's clients.
- A clear understanding of your responsibilities and duties.

Debbie, who volunteers at a children's hospital, was unsure about how to encourage her patients to work harder at their rehabilitation until she began reading books on motivating children. "Children with disabilities come to my ward for physical therapy," Debbie says. "I was trained to help in their therapy, but I had trouble getting some of the kids to want to try. Talking to some of the professionals and reading books really helped me to get them to try harder."

Like Debbie, you will find that the information you need is available. Ask your supervisor or other volunteers for advice or further instruction. Also inquire about books or upcoming seminars on the areas you feel weak in. Through self-study, you can gain further insight that will improve your ability to help and encourage others.

LEARNING ABOUT YOUR SOCIAL PROBLEM AREA

"I wanted to help homeless people because I would see so many of them in my city," says Mary, a volunteer at a homeless mission. "I thought their problem was alcoholism and mental illness until I began reading about homelessness. My whole attitude toward them changed when I realized that the primary problem was poverty and lack of low-income housing."

Many volunteers don't understand the true plight of the people they have chosen to help. Some feel that having compassion toward them is enough; others feel that as long as the volunteer organization understands the problem, they don't have to. This thinking is misleading for several reasons. Most importantly, it affects your attitude toward the needy people you serve. Thinking that people are homeless because they are irresponsible hampers your ability to respect them as individuals. Realizing that in most cases they are victims of complex social problems, on the other hand, helps you to identify with their situation and to be truly motivated to help them.

Your understanding also allows you to better help people in need. Literacy tutors who don't understand the social and emotional problems that create obstacles to learning may find it difficult to motivate their students to learn. Understanding the true nature of the problems of those you are tying to assist contributes to the building of trust. This, in turn, may influence others to accept your offer of help.

To help you get a grasp on the facts concerning your chosen area, read the chapters in Part II of this book which apply to the social problem that concerns you. Also consult the For Further Reading section at the end of the book for sources to broaden your knowledge.

LEARNING TO ENCOURAGE
and MOTIVATE OTHERS

The ability to encourage and motivate the people around you is a valuable resource in all facets of your life. To motivate your friends, co-workers, children, and other family members to do their best could be the most important contribution you make to their lives. This is also true for people in need, many of whom have given up any hope for a better future.

People living in crisis situations, whether due to poverty, family abuse, drug addiction, or illiteracy, often feel there is nothing they can do to improve their circumstances. They view their plight as hopeless, their future as bleak and intolerable. Human care organizations can help them meet their immediate needs, but getting them to believe in themselves and the possibility of a brighter future is an important part of a longer-term solution to their problems.

Volunteers are in a unique position to help them gain that needed hope and self-esteem. Whether working one-on-one with an elderly person or an abandoned child, or assisting in an organization's office doing clerical work, volunteers can interact with the needy in such a way that they make an impression that says, "I am here to help because I care about you as a person."

This section will help you more effectively convey your feelings of concern and caring to the needy person you serve, and give you helpful tips on how to encourage others to rise above their circumstances.

Encouragement

Every contact you as a volunteer have with the people your organization is trying to help is an opportunity to encourage and motivate them. Even while performing duties in which your exposure to the agency's clients is limited, such as fundraising or office work, things you do and say during your brief contacts can help. A warm smile directed at any person can be encouraging, especially to the needy.

Winifred Brown, executive director of the Mayor's Voluntary Action Center in New York, talks about encouraging the needy. "The homeless say people can make them feel like they don't exist. You can be sitting in Grand Central during rush hour, and thousands of people will walk by and act as if you were not there, like you were invisible," she says. "That one person who is able to look them in the eye and smile means so much to them, for it lets them know that they do exist."

Lori, who works with women seeking to turn away from lives of prostitution or drug abuse, says she uses every opportunity she can to encourage others. "I know my visits to the courthouse lock-up may not change the world, but they could plant or nurture an idea in some of the women to seek help." Toni, who volunteers in a hospital and at a homeless mission, says volunteers have to learn to reach out. "They [the volunteers] have to learn to say, hey, you look great today! Give them a pat or a hug; hugs are wonderful!" she adds.

While doing your volunteer work, take the time to say hello and ask about the well-being of your agency's clients. Tell them about their positive characteristics. Inspire them, using your experiences as examples, to try to improve their situation. Listen to their problems and concerns, and encourage them to use the resources available to them, such as professional counseling, legal assistance, and tutoring.

Listening

The ability to listen is key in helping and encouraging any person in need. In many cases, a person's low self-worth is partly due to a feeling that no cares about how he feels or what he thinks. Jim, a homeless man in Santa Cruz asks, "How can anyone know what my problems are if no one listens to me?"

Deb Ridgway, volunteer coordinator at a Chicago advocacy agency, CESO, talks about the importance of listening in working with the homeless. "They [the homeless] come into a shelter at night after being on the street for eighteen hours and being treated like crap," she says. "When they come into the shelter, they don't need to be treated like that again. They need a friend. They need to know they will be left alone if they want to be left alone. Or if they want to talk to someone, they know that the volunteer or staff person is there because they care about them. They know they are going to be called by their name, and they are going to be respected."

Deb's comments apply to other people in need as well. They need to know that the volunteer respects and cares about them. The first thing you can do to show others that you care is to listen to what they have to say. Show them you are interested in how they feel and what they think. This is how Pearl, who delivers meals for Meals On Wheels, shows those she serves her affection. Even though the large number of homebound elderly she serves keeps Pearl on a tight schedule, Pearl will stay and talk if they seem to want company. "I wish I had more time to spend with them," she says.

Sharing Your Life Experiences

Once people feel that you are truly concerned about them, they are much more likely to hear what you have to say. People in need, however, have received more than their share of criticism and unconstructive advice, and they question others' sincerity towards them as a result. For your words to make a difference, they must make it past the individual's listening barriers.

Christine Franklin of the Massachusetts Bay United Way talks about the difficulty of trying to reach the less fortunate. "It is a very tough reach. You have no way of knowing the difficulties they have suffered," she says. "Whether they are disabled, abused, or homeless, many of them feel like you have no way of being where they have been."

One of the best ways to reach someone who is living in difficult circumstances is to talk about yourself and the difficulties you have experienced. Tell the needy person what you did when you were in situations similar to theirs. Nothing can break down barriers faster than the sharing of your own vulnerability and human frailty.

This technique of helping others through the sharing of experiences is at the core of the Alcoholics Anonymous and other Twelve-Step recovery programs. Millions of Americans are recovering from alcoholism, drug addiction, over-eating, and other ailments through these programs. Sharing common experiences removes the barriers separating the long-time recovering alcoholic and the practicing alcoholic. The practicing alcoholic be-

Learning to Listen

Like most Mental Health Association chapters across the country, the MHA of Evanston, Illinois has always been dedicated to promoting mental health, preventing mental illness, advocating rights of the mentally ill, and educating the community about issues of mental health. Ten years ago, their belief in the importance of active listening in volunteer work led to a course designed especially for prospective volunteers.

"Active Listening Skills" is open to anyone wanting to volunteer at human service agencies in Evanston. In the course, skills are divided into six areas: use of silence, attending behavior, verbal following, identifying and reflecting feelings, use of questions, and summarizing. Each is studied and practiced separately to stress the importance of each component. "This may be difficult and feel awkward," reads the course manual, "but we hope that this approach will make you aware of how common conversational responses can become intentional communication tools for use in your volunteer work."

Team-taught by Evanston psychology and social work professionals, the course uses lecture, discussion, role playing, and home practice to pack a lot of information into just six weeks of training. In addition to listening skills, the class also offers information on volunteer rights and responsibilities, an introduction to human care agencies in the community, and an informal forum for sharing questions and concerns about the prospect of volunteering.

"I still have a long way to go," says one new Listening Skills grad. "I still do too much advice-giving when I should be trying to get the other person to figure out things for himself. But just being aware of that has made me a better volunteer already — and a better friend, too."

comes hopeful when he or she sees that people who once were in similar circumstances are now leading normal lives.

LEARNING TO ADVOCATE FOR THE DISADVANTAGED

Unfortunately, there are limits to what we can do as volunteers. While we can help feed, clothe, inspire, teach or comfort, we cannot fix society's structural defects. Problems such as the shortage of low-income housing, the lack of adequate job skills training programs, or the public's attitude toward the disadvantaged must be addressed on a governmental or corporate level.

As a volunteer you can, however, help begin solving these larger issues by becoming advocates. By speaking out, using your vote, and writing letters to legislators, volunteers can bring into the open issues important to those in need. A volunteer who works with the elderly might advocate against cuts in Medicare or Social Security. A volunteer who helps abused children might vote for more funding for his or her local child protection agency. A volunteer who works with teens or illiterate adults could get involved in campaigns to improve local schools.

Whatever the issue, if it concerns the welfare of those you are volunteering to help, you should be involved in some way. This involvement can be as simple as writing a letter or as involved as joining a grassroots campaign seeking positive change. In either case, by embracing the concerns of the needy as your own, you will be making a significant contribution toward alleviating the root causes of their suffering.

The following suggestions outline a simple and non-time-consuming strategy for effecting change:

1) *Vote with the less fortunate in mind.* In most cases, voters are concerned with issues that directly affect them or their families. To be an advocate, however, we must find out where political candidates stand on social issues and policies that have an impact on the people we volunteer for. You can get this information by reading the newspapers or a candidate's position paper, which can be obtained free of charge from the candidate's office. Another way of getting information is by reviewing the candidate's rating on particular issues, which are provided by some

advocacy groups. Americans for Democratic Action, for instance, rates national candidates on their records and stands on many social issues. Local candidates may be rated by a variety of local advocacy groups. With this information, you can cast an "informed" vote — one that will benefit both you and the disadvantaged.

2) *Share your knowledge.* Once you have obtained this information, share it with others. Your fellow volunteers may not be aware of where a candidate stands on important social issues; your friends and family members may not even be aware of how certain political and social issues affect disadvantaged people you care about. Use your knowledge and compassion to win them over, increasing your candidate's base of support.

3) *Write a letter.* Very few constituents, consumers or readers write letters. So when a letter is received by a corporation, politician, or the media, it carries a disproportionate amount of weight. All of those groups, especially politicians, are concerned about public opinion; they read and respond to the mail they receive. Representative Morris Udall of Arizona says he reads every letter sent to him. He also stated that on numerous occasions a letter from a constituent influenced his thinking on a issue.

Pick an issue that concerns the people you volunteer for and write a letter to the appropriate person. For example, to show your support for a program to increase low-income housing, you could write a letter to your mayor's office or local alderman or councilman. To support legislation for a national program, such as AIDS research or Headstart, letters can be sent to your representative or senator.

4) *Support socially responsible companies.* This tactic and its negative counterpart, boycotting, have been used very successfully by the environmental movement. The strategy is to purchase the products of companies which donate generously to charity, promote the volunteer efforts of their employees, improve the communities in which they are located, and provide equal opportunity to the women and minorities they employ.

Of course, this type of information can be difficult to obtain, but there are ways. The Council on Economic Priorities, for instance, rates major corporations on twelve criteria, including the level of charitable donations and the percentage of women and minorities in upper management. They publish their ratings in *Shopping for a Better World*, which is available in most bookstores. You can learn about the activities of local companies through newsletters published by volunteer and social organizations. If you do decide to purchase a company's products because it is socially aware, write the company a letter encouraging it to keep up the good work.

5) *Get other organizations involved.* Encourage the organization you volunteer for, your church, and any other group you may be involved in to support the cause of those in need. By sharing your understanding of and passion for particular issues, you can generate additional votes and letters for your cause.

Unfortunately, the experience of the 1980s has taught us that volunteering by itself is not enough—it must be accompanied by a sympathetic public policy. Volunteers must use their voices, their votes, and their pens to effect fundamental changes for the unfortunate Americans we care so deeply about.

ENCOURAGING OTHERS TO VOLUNTEER

As a volunteer, you are an "ambassador" for volunteerism. More people come to volunteering through someone they know than by any other way. Whether they are family or friends, you can encourage others to help people in need and, in the process, help themselves.

The easiest way to get people to volunteer is by simply asking them. Forty percent of the volunteers surveyed in a recent Gallup Poll said the reason they began volunteering is because someone they knew asked them. People may not respond to advertisements, but they do respond to a family member, neighbor, or friend.

Through asking, Mark has gotten his family involved in volunteering. His mother now teaches a sewing class at the mission where Mark works, while one of his sisters comes to play with the children. Even his "yuppie sister" cooks for the mission every once in a while. Nadja got a group of eight people from her church to visit a nursing home with her once a week. Pearl, whose husband originally thought her volunteering was "silly," now volunteers with her.

Encouraging others to volunteer is an important function

that all volunteers should perform. The need for volunteers has never been greater. In return, you can be sharing the joys of service with your family and friends.

MAKING A DIFFERENCE

As you grow into becoming a more effective volunteer through your experience, continued self-learning, and agency training, you will begin to see a difference in how you respond to various volunteering situations. You will know the right thing to say or do to help. You will find yourself not only meeting the immediate needs of the people you serve, but also imparting the encouragement and motivation that can give a needy person hope and a greater self-esteem.

CHAPTER SIX

Maintaining the Volunteer Spirit

ALTHOUGH THE BENEFITS volunteers receive from their efforts are great, volunteering work itself can be difficult at times. Volunteers are sometimes required to work in unpleasant environments, performing duties that are so stressful and emotionally taxing that most outsiders would wonder why anyone would ever want to do them, let alone for free. But most volunteers are willing and prepared to do that kind of work. What they *aren't* prepared for, however, is having to deal with the personal conflicts within the organizations they are supporting, the lack of feedback on their work, and, even worse, the apathetic or hostile attitude of some of those they are trying to help. More than a few eager volunteers, quickly zapped of their initial energy and enthusiasm, have quit their volunteer jobs within days of starting; a number have been so disillusioned that they have given up volunteering altogether.

Nevertheless, there are millions of volunteers across the country who faithfully carry out their volunteer duties a couple of times a week, and most have been doing it for a long time. They will be the first to agree that the work is not always easy, that there are times when they get frustrated and tired, and that there are nights when the last thing they feel like doing is volunteer work. Yet, they do it because they have learned how to deal with the realities of volunteering and how to maintain their spirit, dedication, and enthusiasm over the long haul.

In this chapter we will look at some of the frustrations volunteers most frequently face and how you as a volunteer can successfully resolve them.

DISILLUSIONMENT

After completing her literacy training program, Kathleen was excited about beginning tutoring lessons with her first student. But barely a month had gone by when Kathleen had lost most of her enthusiasm and was ready to quit, not because the work was so demanding, but because her student wasn't really interested in learning how to read. "All she wanted was for me to take her to get ice cream," Kathleen says. Fortunately, Kathleen continued to work with her student, successfully encouraging her to take an interest in learning to read.

Jean's first volunteering assignment at a homeless shelter was to spend one night a month there, manning the front desk and handing out towels and linens to the guests. The work was easy enough, and Jean would have enjoyed it if it had not been for

---

Rights and Responsibilities of a Volunteer

Rights
1. To be offered the opportunity to be a volunteer
2. To be carefully interviewed and carefully assigned
3. To be carefully supervised
4. To be involved in planning and evaluation
5. To do meaningful and interesting work
6. To be regarded as a person

Responsibilities:
1. To be open and honest with your supervisor from the beginning
2. To understand commitments of time and tasks and to fulfill them
3. To work for acceptance and respect from the staff
4. To participate in evaluation when asked to do so
5. To share thoughts and feelings with staff
6. To respect confidentiality
7. To seek honest feedback
8. To serve as an ambassador of goodwill for the agency
9. To be an effective advocate for change when it is needed
10. To bring the priceless gift of enthusiasm and service which lightens the load of all

Source, Marlene Wilson, in a speech delivered to the Voluntary Action Center, October 31, 1975, on the subject of "Volunteerism: Putting It All Together." Used with permission.

one particularly unruly guest and the chronic understaffing at the mission. Unable to tolerate it, she quit working at the mission after four months. "It got to be a hassle," she says. "I didn't feel like I was really making a difference anyway."

When volunteers like Kathleen and Jean first sign on with service organizations, they come to their jobs with certain expectations—that they will quickly make a difference in the lives of others, that they will be appreciated for their efforts (especially by the people they are helping), and that the organization will have created a structure to support those efforts. Unfortunately, it doesn't always work out that way. Often, volunteers' expectations are not met immediately, leaving them disillusioned and frustrated.

To reduce the possibility of becoming disillusioned early in your volunteering career, it is important that you have realistic expectations of what you can accomplish, that you have a proper perspective on the value of your efforts, and that you realize that it will take time for you to accomplish your volunteering goals.

PATIENCE IN VOLUNTEERING

At first it may be difficult for volunteers to truly appreciate the situations of the people they are trying to help. The needy have led difficult lives, lives that have made many of them bitter, embarrassed, and distrustful, even of the people who are trying to help them. This was especially apparent to Rich, an attorney who does free legal work for the disadvantaged in Minneapolis. "They [the clients] are coming in here because they have nowhere else to go, but there is a lot of resentment," he says. "The vast majority have a feeling they are going to get screwed."

Like many volunteers, Rich has found that he needs to take the time to prove himself to the needy, to show that he cares about them and has their best interests at heart. For some volunteers, proving themselves has been just a matter of showing up regularly for their volunteer assignments. The people can see how dedicated you are, and they equate your concern with your dedication. But many of the needy demand more active signs of your concern before they will allow you to help them. They will notice if you are making a real effort to get to know them. Like any relationship, those you establish with the needy will grow with time, with conversation, with a sharing of your personal life and your own problems.

To help others, the volunteer must be patient. Accepting help demands that the needy lower their pride and become vulnerable. It will take time for many of them to come to trust you and feel comfortable accepting your help. Christine Franklin of the United Way stresses how important it is for volunteers to have that patience. "It can be very frustrating for volunteers that they cannot immediately interject themselves into someone's life," she says. "It takes time. Many people will not allow you to help them immediately."

Putting Your Value Into Perspective

Another source of disillusionment is feeling that one's volunteering efforts aren't making a difference in the lives of others. Seeing the same homeless people coming into a mission day after day with no foreseeable resolution of their plight can be extremely frustrating. What the volunteer must realize is that there are advocates and legislators working to solve the homeless problem, and that the volunteer's task is to help the homeless survive by providing them with food, shelter and hope until a longer-term solution can be found. In order to impart hope to the people they serve, volunteers must be able to put into perspective how their work is important, and realize that their efforts are part of a larger plan to help alleviate the problem.

To keep things in perspective, ask yourself what would happen if all the people doing volunteer work were to quit. What would happen to homeless people if missions closed for lack of volunteers? What if all literacy tutors or hotline counselors quit? Would the people in need be worse off? By asking yourself questions like these, the value of your individual service may become more apparent.

AVOIDING VOLUNTEER BURNOUT

People often volunteer out of a compassion for people who are less fortunate. Too much compassion or determination to make a difference, however, can greatly impair a volunteer's ability to be effective. Too many volunteers have burned out or overloaded themselves emotionally by trying to do too much or by assuming personal responsibility for the suffering of others.

You Cannot Solve the Problem Alone

You want to help others, but if your efforts are to be successful, they must first want to help themselves. Toni, a 14-year veteran at the Metrohelp Runaway Hotline, advises new volunteers this way: "You can empathize, sympathize, be supportive, but it is still their problem. You can give them all the tools in the world to work with, but you cannot do it for them."

Ashley, a crisis counselor, agrees with Toni. "You have to keep yourself from getting too involved," she says. "You can't dwell on every caller—you have to learn to separate yourself." Ashley says the agency she works for has a volunteering philosophy. "When you come to the agency, you don't think about your problems: you think about the callers. Then when you leave, you leave their problems at the hotline and pick up your own."

To help others, you must be able to separate yourself from their problems. Though you want to do all you can to help, you cannot take responsibility for their situation or its resolution.

Don't Overcommit Yourself

Sometimes well-meaning volunteers want to immerse themselves in their work, and as a consequence, commit too much time and energy at the expense of their other activities. Ashley talks about how she burned out by taking on too much responsibility. "They [the crisis line supervisors] didn't have a lot of volunteers at the time, so I was working thirty to forty hours a month, working extra shifts and helping new volunteers." Ashley found the other parts of her life getting out of balance and she was increasingly stressed, until she cut back her volunteering to one day a week.

Like Ashley, volunteers must realize that there is a limit to the time and energy they have to invest into their volunteer work if they are to be effective. They must also be willing to share with other volunteers the burden of helping and realize they don't have to—and can't—do it all.

OVERCOMING ORGANIZATIONAL FRUSTRATIONS

Working in any structured environment can lead to frustration, and it is no different in non-profit agencies. Interacting with su-

---

Lutheran Volunteer Corps

When people begin looking for a full-time commitment to volunteering, a few names usually pop up. Peace Corps, which promotes world peace and helps developing countries achieve greater self-sufficiency, and VISTA, which serves domestic communities, are two large, well-known, and worthy programs. But scattered throughout the country are other challenging opportunities that are just a little harder to find. One of these is Lutheran Volunteer Corps.

Headquartered in Washington, D.C., Lutheran Vopunteer Corps (LVC) is a one- and two-year service program open to adults of all Christian faith traditions. As with Peace Corps and VISTA, working for social justice is a big part of the LVC, but two equally important emphases are living a simpler lifestyle and living in intentional Christian communities. "It really is something that is a little different from Peace Corps or VISTA," says one LVC staff member. She calls it "a challenge to put faith and lifestyle together."

Service areas include Baltimore, Chicago, Milwaukee, Washington, D.C., and Wilmington, Delaware. Agencies which use LVC volunteers range from food banks and health care centers to educational centers and political activism agencies, such as the Illinois Nuclear Weapons Freeze Campaign. Before it can be accepted, a placement site is evaluated according to standards of social justice concerns and volunteer needs. Volunteers are only placed in situations of significant challenge and responsibility. Their positions range from community workers to education coordinators to lobbyists and beyond.

In addition to coordinating volunteer interests with the needs of LVC-approved agencies, LVC also provides transportation to the volunteer's chosen city, a subsistence salary, medical insurance, living quarters in small, intentional Christian communities, and a support committee.

pervisors, paid staff members, and other volunteers can be difficult, as can dealing with an organization's operating philosophy.

In voluntary organizations, having both the paid staff and
volunteers working together can be a source of conflict. The paid
workers may question the wisdom of using untrained volunteers
in certain jobs. A few full-timers may even be concerned about
their own job security when the agency uses volunteers in positions they feel should go to paid professionals. The personalities
of the paid workers may conflict with your own. Your supervisor
may underestimate your abilities or commitment and assign you
to unchallenging and mundane tasks.

Some agencies are reluctant to include volunteers in planning
or feedback sessions or to accept volunteer input. They may
not give their volunteers adequate guidance or feedback on
their efforts. The sources of organizational frustration can indeed be numerous. Among the most common complaints by
volunteers include:

—Too much supervision
—Not enough supervision
—Not enough responsibility
—Inadequate training for task assigned
—Vague organizational goals and policies
—Lack of feedback on volunteer progress or efforts
—Unclear job definition or supervisory relationships
—Lack of acceptance of volunteer input or ideas

Resolving Organizational Conflicts

To avoid these conflicts, find out before you sign up with an
agency exactly how the organization and its staff view the role of
its volunteers. That kind of information is not always given in
your interview, so if it is not mentioned, ask your interviewer. Be
wary of accepting a position with an organization if its views
don't coincide with yours.

When a conflict arises, try to identify the exact cause of your
frustration before talking to your supervisor. Is it that you don't

feel appreciated for your efforts? Or is that you feel the agency hasn't given you enough responsibility? Does it revolve around a personality conflict or is it a reflection of your uncertainty about your job responsibilities?

Once you have located the cause of your frustrations, discuss it with your supervisor or administrator. Volunteer agencies are concerned about keeping their workers happy, both volunteers and paid staff; if you have a problem, they will want to hear about it. Only then can they take steps to resolve your frustration.

If over a period of time, however, your frustrations with the organization are not resolved, discuss your situation with a clearinghouse counselor. The answer may be that you aren't in the right volunteering job. An unbiased volunteer counselor can best help you decide what recourse you have.

MAINTAINING THE VOLUNTEER SPIRIT

The benefits of volunteering don't always come cheap, and the price sometimes includes dealing with frustrations and hassles. Maintaining a volunteer spirit requires patience, understanding, and sometimes a lot of conversation. But for millions of volunteers, the effort has been well worth it.

PART II

Social Service Agenda

CHAPTER SEVEN

The American Homeless

VALERIE, her husband and their four children were once a happy family, living contentedly in a quiet Brooklyn neighborhood. Although Valerie's husband's earnings as a factory worker were modest, they always seemed to get by. But when he developed a drinking problem, things began to change. He became violent, abusing both Valerie and the children whenever he got drunk or angry. Fearing for their own safety, Valerie and the children moved out. Suddenly without a place to live or any means of support, they turned to the Department of Human Services, which placed them in a hotel for the homeless.

Jim is an intelligent and insightful middle-age man. His grasp of American history and his understanding of current social and economic issues is impressive, and he proposes reasonable solutions to many of our more complex social problems. Jim is homeless, living in the streets of Santa Cruz, California. He receives monthly Social Security checks and sleeps in the park when the weather is good, retreating to the city's shelters when it rains or turns cold. He looks for jobs from time to time but has only been offered ones he claims are "beneath my educational background and experience." Jim is not an alcoholic, but his mental stability is questionable.

Mike, Joanne and their two children were a lower middle-income family until Mike was laid off when automobile plant closings nationwide forced thousands out of work in the early 1980s. After his layoff, both he and Joanne took low-paying service jobs, but Joanne had to quit when she became pregnant. Mike took a second job, but still unable to keep pace with the increasing cost of living, he fell heavily into debt. When Mike missed his mortgage payments, the savings and loan bank foreclosed on his home and the family was forced to move out. With no place to go, they lived in their station wagon for a few weeks until they could find temporary shelter.

Valerie, Jim, and Mike are part of the estimated 650,000 to 3.5 million Americans who make up the homeless, a diverse group which includes single adults, families, teenagers and children. Among their ranks are single-parent families on welfare, alcoholics, battered women and children, the mentally ill, runaway teens, Vietnam Veterans and blue-collar workers financially devastated by the loss of manufacturing jobs in their cities.

THE MEANING OF HOMELESSNESS

To most of us, to be homeless means to be without shelter. To those who are homeless, however, it means much more. It means living in fear, not knowing where your next meal will come from or where you will spend the night. It means living in shame, feeling that you have failed yourself and your family. Alienated from family and friends, the homeless are relegated to a life totally dependent on the generosity of strangers, social agencies, and volunteers for survival.

The homeless are at the mercy of the streets. As a group, they are much more likely to be the victims of crime or substance abuse. Homeless women are twenty times more likely to be sexually assaulted than other women, and youths that are homeless have the highest rates of pregnancy, alcoholism and drug abuse of any adolescent group.

While the lack of shelter and proper diet contributes to the poor physical health of the homeless, uncertainty and fear impacts their mental health. Homeless children suffer from both physical and psychological disorders at rates ten times those of other children. As many as one-third of homeless adults suffer from chronic illnesses or trauma.

The true meaning of homelessness is something that most of us have difficulty even imagining. But for some unfortunate people, it is a harsh reality. Creola, a homeless woman in Baltimore trying to explain what her life was like, told a reporter, "I stayed on the streets, sometimes in empty houses for three months. It was terrible. I was scared. But I had no place else to go."

WHO ARE THESE HOMELESS AMERICANS?

Homelessness affects people of every race, gender, and age. While most prevalent among the poor, it has touched even middle-income Americans. In a reader survey conducted by *Money Magazine,* 23% of those responding indicated they have considered the possibility that they themselves might become homeless. They realize that unforseen disasters, such as a financial crisis or medical emergency, can happen to anyone.

The homeless represent a wide spectrum of the American population. Below is a description of five groups that make up the majority of the homeless:

Single-Parent Families Headed by Women

Families, especially those headed by single women, are the fastest growing segment of the homeless population. Many of

---

Deborah's Place

On the near Northside of Chicago a small shelter, Deborah's Place, gives homeless women a place to go. In a city with over 350,000 homeless people, the shelter's thirty beds may not seem like much. But for the thousands of women who have stayed there, it's a very special place.

"I love this shelter," says Amanda, a seventy-five-year-old homeless woman. "It's different from the other ones because there aren't any men, and they let the girls use the refrigerator. You know, in the summer time the girls like a nice cold drink. They are nice girls here."

For many women like Amanda, a women's shelter is a luxury. Because of the high rate of sexual assault on homeless women, the fear of men is overwhelming; many of them prefer to stay in the street rather than go to shelters which also accept men.

Deborah's Place, one of the two women's overnight shelters in Chicago, gives homeless women a safe and comfortable place to live. It's a place to rebuild their lives and help them regain their independence and ability to function in society.

Source, "They Call Themselves The Lucky Ones" by Marney Keenan, *Chicago Tribune.* Copyrighted, Chicago Tribune Company. All rights reserved. Used with permission.

these women are on public aid, while others became homeless after fleeing violent and abusive spouses. While families headed by single women comprise approximately 25% of the nation's homeless population, they make up over 80% of the homeless in Massachusetts and New York City. Their ranks exceed 50% of the homeless population in Atlanta and Denver.

Homeless Children

Dr. Ellen Bassuck, an authority on the homeless, estimates that there are some 750,000 homeless children. Half of them are under five years of age; many are infants. In New York City alone, at least 800 infants go without sufficient food, clothing, health care or shelter every day.

While the majority of homeless children live with their parents, nearly 5% of them are on their own, living off the streets. These are the runaway teenagers and abandoned children, the so-called "throwaway kids" who often turn to prostitution, theft, and selling drugs for survival.

The Mentally Ill Homeless

Many Americans, including former President Reagan, believe that mental illness is the primary cause of homelessness. Reagan blames the problem on the government's programs during the 1970s which deinstitutionalized many mental patients who weren't homicidal, suicidal, or dangerous to others. Reagan is partially correct: over 25% of the homeless population is mentally unstable. Studies of homeless individuals living in shelters in Washington, Boston, and Philadelphia found that between 36% and 39% of those surveyed suffer from schizophrenia. In addition, a 1988 study of homeless people in Los Angeles reported that 44% of them had prior psychiatric hospitalization.

Homeless Veterans

It is estimated that as many as 500,000 homeless men are veterans, most of them from the Vietnam War. Many suffer from alcoholism, drug-addiction, and mental disorders, illnesses in many cases directly related to their involvement in combat.

Homeless veterans are not a new phenomenon in this country. Both the Civil War and World War I produced large populations of homeless veterans.

Two-Parent Families

A small percentage of the homeless is made up of lower middle-income working families who were caught in a severe economic crunch caused by job layoffs, expensive illnesses, or fires. They lacked an adequate support system of family, friends, and savings to which they could turn in their time of need. Fortunately, the average length of homelessness for this group is relatively short: less than a year, according to one report.

CAUSES OF HOMELESSNESS

There are a number of factors that influence homelessness. Although poverty and the lack of adequate low-income housing are the primary causes, family breakdowns, substance abuse, the deinstitutionalization of the mentally ill, and the loss of traditional manufacturing jobs contribute greatly to the problem. Below is an overview of the role each of these issues plays in the homeless crisis.

Lack of Affordable Housing

One of the major problems facing the homeless is the steep decline in the availability of low-income housing. During the Carter and Ford administrations, 500,000 federally subsidized, low-income housing units were constructed; during the Reagan administration, only 25,000 units were built. Since 1981, annual funding for federal housing assistance programs has declined from $32 billion to less than $8 billion. In major cities across the country, half a million low-income housing units are lost to condominium conversion, arson, demolition and abandonment each year. The number of single-room occupancy units, the primary residence of many of the mentally ill who were deinstitutionalized during the 1970s, has decreased by 50% due to construction of luxury apartments and office buildings.

Poverty

The number of people in this country whose income falls below the poverty level has increased by 27%, or seven million people since 1979. This increase in poverty can be partially attributed to the cutback in federal government spending on social programs. Spending on social programs decreased from 25.5% of the federal budget in 1980 to 18.3% in 1987. A recent study by the

---

The New Homeless

In response to the rapidly increasing number of families, women, children and adolescents without shelter, the Association of Junior Leagues and the Johnson Foundation sponsored a forum titled, "The New Homeless: Women, Children and Families." Held in October of 1987, the forum included fifty participants (including social service professionals, homeless advocates, university researchers, policy makers and Junior League members) who came together to examine the causes of homelessness. They also drafted an "Agenda for Action" with recommendations for changes in public policy to help alleviate the homeless problem.

During the forum, participants presented research showing the seriousness of the plight of the new homeless. Their presentations highlighted the following statistics:

- In 1987, single women accounted for an estimated 25% of the homeless population, up from 10% in 1982.
- As many as 33% of the homeless population is made up of families, either women with children or two-parent families.
- As many as one-third of homeless people are children under the age of eighteen.
- The number of homeless families, women, and children is growing at a rate of 25% a year.

The forum participants also discussed the many causes of the rapid growth of the new homeless. Some of the causes highlighted include: lack of affordable housing, family breakdowns, domestic violence, poverty, and inadequate public aid benefits.

During the last session of the forum, the participants developed an Agenda for Action which included both short- and long-term strategies which, combining both the government and the private sector in partnership, could alleviate the homeless problem. The Agenda

Center on Budget and Policy Priorities showed that the buying power of monthly public aid grants has declined by more than 50% since 1970. In describing the plight of the homeless families she had interviewed, Dr. McChesney, a professor of sociology studying the homeless, says, "These families became homeless because they were poor. They had been poor long before they became homeless, and often had been barely making it for some time."

The New Homeless—Continued

for Action was a comprehensive document recommending action in six areas. The following is an overview of some of these recommendations:

Housing: Increase low-income housing, improve shelter facilities, and increase rent subsidies.

Community Education: Conduct public awareness programs to dispel the myths about who the homeless are and to raise the visibility of the new homeless.

Education, Training and Job Placement: Promote literacy programs for adults, ensure that homeless children can attend school, and develop job training programs for the homeless.

Economic Security: Reform welfare programs, increase public aid benefit levels for families with children, increase work incentives for AFDC recipients, raise the minimum wage, and extend unemployment benefits.

Social Services: Expand programs for child care, strengthen community and family support programs, develop foster care programs for older youths, create counseling programs for the homeless.

Physical and Mental Health: Create an adequate follow-up system for the mentally ill, expand alcohol and drug rehabilitation programs, increase Medicaid eligibility, establish health programs for homeless children and adolescents.

From *The New Homeless: Women, Children and Families. An Issues Forum On The Homeless.* The Association of Junior Leagues. Copyright 1988. Used with permission.

The economic problems facing the poor are compounded by the increasing cost of low-income housing. In 1985, almost 50% of the nation's poor spent at least 70% of their incomes on housing. In Boston, for example, a family with five children received welfare benefits of $654 per month in 1986, while the average monthly rent for a two-bedroom apartment was over $660.

Family Breakdown

The rapid growth in the number of homeless single-parent families and children is due in part to an increase in family violence and divorce. Many women and their children become homeless after fleeing a violent spouse. Similarly, teenagers often find themselves on the street after fleeing from abusive parents or other family problems. In one study which examined the characteristics of homeless families, researchers found that almost one-third of the families surveyed became homeless due to a battering, the death or illness of a mate, or the dissolution of a relationship.

Deinstitutionalization of Mental Patients

During the 1960s and 1970s, over 300,000 mental patients were released from institutions because of new laws which made involuntary commitments to mental institutions more difficult. A support system of neighborhood residential centers and mental health out-patient clinics was to be established. However, when the mental patients were released, they had no place to go because most of the promised residential centers had never been built. The existing out-patient clinic system was unable to handle the increased demand. No one knows exactly what happened to the former patients who were not accommodated by these centers, but a number of them became part of the homeless population.

In a report to Congress in 1986, the director of the National Institute of Mental Health said that 937,300 diagnosed schizophrenics were released from mental institutions. Their whereabouts are now unknown.

Loss of Traditional Jobs

Since 1980, traditional, well-paying jobs in the manufacturing industries, such as automobile, steel, and machine parts, have decreased by two million each year. Industrial cities such as Detroit, Pittsburgh, Gary, Buffalo, and Houston were the hardest hit. Laid-off workers from these cities were forced to move away from families and friends to look for work elsewhere. Of those that did eventually find work, roughly half had to take jobs at

Homeless Volunteers: Jean and Mark

Jean and Mark both work as volunteers at homeless missions, Jean as an overnight monitor at a men's shelter, and Mark as a tutor for children at a shelter for homeless families. Although their jobs are very different, they both feel it is important that prospective volunteers know about both the joy and difficulty of working with the homeless.

Jean says that she has found her work as a monitor extremely fulfilling. "It's unfortunate that there are so many nice people whose circumstances caused them to become homeless. You would really be surprised at how events can lead people with previously normal lives to homelessness," she explains. Jean says that talking to some of them gave her a new perspective on how unimportant material things in life really are.

Working at the shelter was frustrating at times for Jean because of under-staffing and the occasional unruly guest. "This one guy would threaten to burn down the mission. He made it difficult for me to sleep through the night."

After four months, Jean decided to find other ways to help the homeless. "I was spending two nights a month because of the under-staffing. I was having a difficult time at work the next day because I didn't sleep well at the mission." She knew it was time for a change when she found herself thinking, "If I have to hear another macho hard luck story, I'm going to go crazy." Jean now volunteers at a mission for homeless women, which she finds much more fulfilling.

Mark volunteers once a week to tutor and play with children at a residential program for battered homeless women and their children. Mark says he enjoys his volunteering. "You could be having an awful day, but when you go to the shelter, you feel really good coming out."

The most difficult thing for Mark is seeing the injuries the kids have suffered at the hands of their fathers. "Once, a mother came in with a broken leg, the kid had a broken arm and kept saying how much he missed his daddy," Mark said. "You wonder why the hell this goes on."

poverty-level wages; some who couldn't find work at all became homeless.

PUBLIC POLICY TO COMBAT HOMELESSNESS

In 1988 Congress passed the McKinney Homeless Assistance Amendment Act, a federal bill granting aid to the homeless. For fiscal year 1989, the act allocated $635 million dollars to fund emergency food and shelter programs, mental health programs, alcohol and substance abuse programs, and health, education and job training programs. The McKinney Act also allows the Department of Health and Human Services to lease vacant federal properties to agencies to be converted into shelters for the homeless.

State and local governments are also developing programs to attack the homeless problem. New York has established welfare hotels and opened huge armories to house New York City's large homeless population. Vacant city-owned buildings are being rehabilitated to provide permanent housing for the city's homeless. Project Help, a state-funded organization, sends out vans to deliver psychiatric and medical care to the state's mentally ill homeless.

In Florida, the state legislature appropriated $15 million for emergency grants to homeless families and local agencies serving the homeless. The New Jersey legislature funded a $2.8 million dollar program that provides loans to people facing eviction. In Houston, the school system opens its gyms to homeless teens, while the Emergency Housing Service in Seattle provides emergency shelter and transitional housing for that city's homeless. Across the country, state and local governments are addressing the needs of their homeless population by appropriating funds for them.

Yet the problem still appears far from being solved. Relatively few funds are being appropriated to solve the problem of the lack of affordable housing. And despite of the increased funding for emergency shelters, a January 1989 study by the U.S. Conference of Mayors found that in 75% of the cities surveyed, the homeless are still being turned away from shelters due to overcrowding.

VOLUNTEERING TO COMBAT HOMELESSNESS

Much of the work to improve the lives of the nation's homeless is being done by numerous not-for-profit organizations that are staffed mainly by volunteers. The types of programs offered by large national organizations and local church and community groups alike vary greatly, but they can be classified by function: missions and shelters, feeding programs, advocacy groups, outreach programs, and housing programs.

Missions and Shelters

Missions provide temporary shelter, food and clothing to the homeless. Some also offer health care, tutoring, counseling, and substance abuse rehabilitation. These shelters, located across the country, can hold as few as ten to as many as 300 people per night. While some are affiliated with national human care organizations, such as The Salvation Army and Catholic Charities, most are run by churches or community-based organizations.

Homeless shelters usually operate from 7:00 p.m. to 7:00 a.m. and provide guests with an evening meal and breakfast. Daytime shelters, called drop-in centers, give the homeless a place to go when the missions are closed. Some of them provide lunch, showers, recreational activities and a place to receive mail.

Shelters rely heavily on volunteers. At some shelters, volunteers spend the night once a month, socializing with guests, preparing the evening meal, and handing out blankets, toothpaste, and other necessities. The next morning, volunteers serve breakfast and straighten up before leaving.

Volunteers who do not want to stay overnight can help prepare meals, do office work, collect food and supplies, organize recreational programs and socialize with guests. They can tutor homeless children or teach job skills to adults. Doctors and nurses can provide medical care, while legal and counseling professionals can assist the homeless in getting public aid and qualifying for housing programs.

Soup Kitchens and Food Pantries

Soup kitchens and food pantries prepare meals for the homeless and other disadvantaged people. Run by churches and community groups, some serve lunch on a specific day of the week, while others serve several meals a day, seven days a week.

Most soup kitchens are small, allowing volunteers the opportunity to sit down and talk with guests. At Cafe 458, an Atlanta soup kitchen, volunteers give emotional support and friendship along with food. Says Reverend Short, one of the founders of Cafe 458, "We're serving more than food here. We're serving friendship, hospitality and brotherhood. We're trying to develop a relationship with people in transition."

Outreach Programs

Many homeless who choose not to go to shelters can still be helped by volunteers through outreach programs. Some programs send groups of volunteers out into the streets to invite homeless people into the shelters. In other programs, volunteers deliver food, clothing and medical services to the homeless wherever they can be found.

Volunteer Activities At The National Coalition For The Homeless

Food Distribution: Volunteers help prepare and hand out sandwiches.

Shelter Monitoring: The shelters run by cities must meet minimum standards. Volunteers monitor shelters, noting working conditions and any violations of standards. Volunteers visit one or more shelters once a week or every other week. Visits last less than two hours.

Legislative Alert System: A phone network of volunteers call their representatives and encourage them to support legislation regarding homeless issues.

Direct Action Network: Volunteers take part in demonstrations, rallies and other direct actions to pressure elected officials, individuals, and institutions to work toward solutions to end homelessness.

Office Volunteering: Volunteers help around the office with mailings, phone work, data entry, and other related office tasks.

Special Needs Volunteering: Volunteers such as writers, doctors, lawyers, CPAs, plumbers, etc., offer their special skills

Adapted from pamphlet by The New York Coalition for the Homeless. Used with permission.

Advocacy

Across the country, groups are being formed to speak on behalf of the homeless. Attacking issues such as poverty, lack of affordable housing, and ineffective governmental programs, advocacy groups speak out against homelessness in America. The largest of these, National Coalition for the Homeless, is a national organization with local branches throughout the country. Other advocacy groups are located in most urban areas.

Volunteers are needed in every capacity. Lawyers, writers and office workers are used to educate and lobby politicians and lawmakers. Volunteers also monitor conditions in government-run shelters.

Housing Programs

Volunteers also help build permanent and transitional housing for the homeless. One national program, Habitat for Humanity, uses both skilled and unskilled volunteers to build or renovate homes for families. This program usually requires volunteers to work two or three Saturdays a month. Other programs run by local organizations rehabilitate shelters, hotels, and other buildings for transitional housing or single-room occupancy units for the homeless.

VOLUNTEERS NEEDED

The homeless problem in America is reaching epidemic proportions. Volunteers are sorely needed to help the homeless survive until longer-term solutions to the problem can be found. Whether spending two hours every week to tutor homeless kids, spending one night a month at a shelter, or collecting blankets and clothes for a nearby shelter, volunteers can make the biggest difference in the fight against homelessness.

CHAPTER EIGHT

Abused and Neglected Children

THE ACCOUNTS of the death of six-year-old Lisa Steinberg in New York City were a grim reminder of the reality of child abuse. Angry at his adoptive daughter Lisa for staring at him, Joel Steinberg beat her into unconsciousness and left her with his lover, Hedda Nussbaum, herself long a victim of Joel's physical abuse. Hedda, afraid of further angering Joel by taking Lisa to the hospital, left the child lying comatose in the bathroom. Never regaining consciousness, Lisa was finally taken to the hospital, where she died a few days later.

Child abuse has traditionally been considered an isolated family problem, but as the literature arising out of Lisa's death has indicated, it's a widespread problem that's getting worse every year. Two million cases of child abuse were reported in 1986, up 12% from the previous year, up an astounding 223% from 1976. Of course, this takes into account only documented cases; no one knows how many cases go unreported, but the number could easily be twice as high.

Also on the rise is the number of children who die from abuse. In 1988, an estimated 1,225 children died from abuse, a 20% increase over the previous year. Of those dying of child abuse, most are infants. Recent surveys in Los Angeles County and the State of Illinois indicate that 75% of the fatally abused victims are under one year of age. Nationwide, homicide, which is almost always due to abuse, is the greatest single cause of injury-related deaths among babies.

WHAT IS CHILD ABUSE?

The term child abuse has primarily been used to refer to physical harm and sexual abuse intentionally taken out on a child, usually by a parent or a close relation or guardian. Of the two million reported cases of child abuse in 1988, the vast majority were physical abuse cases. The injuries suffered most often by the children in these cases include bruises, lacerations, burns, fractures, cuts, and internal injuries.

In recent years, however, the definition of abuse has been broadened to encompass neglect of a child's basic emotional and physical well-being. Included in this category are cruelty, rejection, humiliation, abandonment, malnutrition, and lack of medical care. There are nearly 250,000 reported cases of emotional abuse every year, and some experts believe that child neglect cases may outnumber those of physical abuse by a margin of ten to one.

SOCIAL CAUSES OF CHILD ABUSE

For those of us who grew up in safe, loving homes, it is difficult to understand how a parent or relative could abuse or neglect a child. While child abuse experts believe that marital difficulties, the stress of parenting, and personality disorders can lead to

---

Catholic Charities

Through its child protection, foster care, and adoption services, Catholic Charities is very involved in helping abused and neglected children. Their social workers and volunteers help assist child protection agencies by investigating alleged cases of child abuse, by providing emergency foster care for children, and by licensing foster homes. Catholic Charities also runs shelters for children and provides in-home protective services so that at-risk families can remain intact.

Through its 600 member agencies and institutions, Catholic Charities also runs shelters for homeless adults, alcohol and drug rehabilitation programs, and recreational programs for seniors, in addition to soup kitchens and job training programs.

For volunteers, Catholic Charities, like other large national non-profits, offers hundreds of different opportunities to help the disadvantaged. But for volunteers who want to work with abused children and their families through a national organization, Catholic Charities is most likely the place to call.

child abuse, they have also found that several social factors contribute greatly to the growth of the problem in this country.

Poverty

"Poverty doesn't kill; it sets the stage," says John Goad, administrator of Illinois's Cook Country child-protection services. Goad was referring to research results that point to a strong correlation between child abuse fatalities and poverty. A study of child abuse in New York City found that three out of four fatally abused children came from welfare families. Another nationwide study found that while one out of every fourteen middle-class children is a victim of severe abuse, one out of every nine children from low-income families is abused.

Child abuse experts attribute the greater incidence of abuse among the poor to the additional stresses faced by parents living below the poverty line and the lack of outside help to ease the strain. Dr. Vincent Fontana of the New York Foundling Hospital cites financial stress, unemployment, and over-crowded housing in the inner-cities as contributing factors to the abuse problem.

Drug and Alcohol Abuse

Researchers have also found a strong connection between alcohol and drug addiction and child abuse. Like the Steinberg child abuse case, at least 40% of all abuse cases involve drugs or alcohol. It has been shown that addicted parents are unable to care for and protect their children. A number of studies have shown how a parent's personality can be dramatically changed by drugs, especially crack and cocaine.

Parents Abused as Children

Parents who suffered abuse at the hands of their parents or relatives are six times more likely than other parents to abuse their own children. Two Yale psychologists, Joan Kaufmann and Edward Zigler, concluded from their research that 30% of those who were abused as children will abuse their own offspring.

Many of these parents suffer personality disorders caused by abusive childhoods, such as low self-esteem, suppressed anger, depression, shame, and in more severe cases, multiple personalities. Unable to resolve their past, they pass on their abusive tendencies to their children.

PUBLIC POLICY TO
PREVENT CHILD ABUSE

The primary responsibility of protecting children from abuse falls on the state, county or city child protective service (CPS) agencies. Employing social workers in addition to medical, psychiatric, and other health professionals, CPS agencies are responsible for investigating reports of child abuse and finding foster homes or adoptive parents for children who are at risk.

Unfortunately, these agencies are in the middle of the child abuse controversy. Accused of placing children with abusive foster parents or leaving children in homes where they are eventually harmed or killed, CPS agencies have suffered a credibility problem in recent years.

Although CPS agencies have mishandled some abuse cases, the agencies have not as a rule mismanaged or neglected their

Boarder Babies

The crack epidemic has created a new term, "Boarder Babies." Born to mothers addicted to drugs, these infants are part of a population whose size has swelled in recent years. In New York City alone, more than 300 babies addicted to cocaine are born every month, staying hospitalized until they are detoxified. Following the agony of withdrawal from cocaine, they remain in the hospital, waiting until their parents can be successfully rehabilitated or until foster parents can be found. While the average stay for a Boarder Baby is about thirty days, some remain in the hospital over six months, waiting for a place to be found for them.

Fortunately, a call for help by New York City's hospitals produced an outpouring of support for the city's Boarder Babies. Hundreds of people volunteered to visit the hospitals regularly to care for and share their love with the infants. Another 5,000 families signed up to adopt the babies.

Volunteers in New York City and around the country are helping to ease the pain of babies born addicted. But until the drug epidemic in America subsides, Boarder Babies will continue to reside in the nation's hospitals.

Source, *U.S. News & World Report.* Copyright, U.S. News & World Report, 1988. Used with permission. All rights reserved.

responsibilities, as their critics charge. The major problem is a lack of money. Without money child service organizations are unable to adequately carry out their duties. While the number of reported child abuse cases has risen 55% in the last five years, governmental funding has risen only 2% during the same time period. Consequently, social workers, whose normal load should be fifteen to twenty abuse cases, are handling as many as fifty cases at a time.

A recent study of the Illinois Department of Children and Family Services showed that social workers were monitoring an average of fifty to sixty abused or neglected children at a time. According to the report, this extreme work load contributes to inadequate supervision and quality care for the children. In some cases, children are even "lost" in the system.

Social workers are also negatively impacted by the high caseload. Across the country, social workers are "burning out" and leaving the system in large numbers. Loretta McCarty of the Dallas Child Protective Services agency says that 45% of her agency's case workers left within the last year alone. To make up for the high turnover, agencies are forced to hire inexperienced and undertrained personnel.

To correct these problems, additional funding must be provided by both the state and federal government. Today, CPS agencies are faced with continuing increases in the number of abused and neglected children. They also face new challenges, such as babies addicted to cocaine. Without increased funding to hire additional well-trained and experienced caseworkers, some serious cases of abuse will continue to go undetected.

VOLUNTEER EFFORTS

Outside organizations help relieve the overload on CPS agencies by providing adoption and protection services. The Children's Home Society and Catholic Charities maintain emergency foster homes and offer adoption services, counseling for abusive parents, and in-home protection services to keep troubled families intact. In some cases, Catholic Charities assists state agencies by investigating state-referred child abuse/neglect cases.

Among the largest of the organizations addressing the issue is the National Committee for The Prevention of Child Abuse

(NCPCA), which is dedicated to reducing child abuse in America by at least 20% by the end of 1991. The NCPCA has established local branches in each state to provide services to parents and children alike. Among the many programs offered are parenting education and support for new parents, crisis counseling for parents under stress, and treatment for abused children. Every year the committee also runs public awareness campaigns, under such slogans as "Words can hit as hard as a fist," which include public service messages in all media. In addition, the NCPCA sponsors Child Abuse Prevention Month every April.

The NCPCA and other organizations whose goals are to reduce child abuse use volunteers extensively. Other ways volunteers can help include:

Working with CPS Agencies

CPS agencies use volunteers to help ease the overload on the professional staff. Working as case aides, office workers, tutors and recreational aides at CPS emergency foster homes, volunteers assist the staff in processing cases and providing care and support to children removed from abusive homes.

Child Abuse Education Programs

These programs work to reduce child abuse by educating parents on proper parenting techniques and by empowering children with the skills and attitudes essential to avoiding victimization. Volunteers working with such organizations as the Boys Club of America or at local community centers teach children how to avoid sexual assault and abuse. Other programs work with teenage mothers and other first-time parents on how to successfully meet their parenting responsibilities. Teachers, counselors, and medical professionals are needed to serve as volunteers.

Child Abuse Prevention Programs

Prevention programs provide crisis and support services for parents under stress or with abusive tendencies. The NCPCA works with a national self-help program for abusive or troubled parents, Parents Anonymous. This program involves over 8,000 volunteers, who serve as counselors and crisis hotline operators.

Some community organizations and local hospitals also offer counseling for these parents. One such organization, Kids Crusaders for Abused Children in Florida, offers weekly respite

"I Think It's A Real Worthy Thing To Do"

When asked why she became a volunteer at FACT (Families and Children in Trouble), Ashley, a research assistant of child psychiatry at the National Institute of Mental Health, says, "I guess the real reason is because of my background and also because I think it's a real worthy thing to do." And the idea of working on a crisis hotline had long interested her. "I've always been intrigued by working with a crisis hotline, although that might sound strange to some people," she says. "A lot of my friends still don't quite understand. They can think of a lot of other things that would not be quite as stressful as working on a crisis hotline."

Ashley's education and professional background have helped prepare her for working on FACT's crisis line. She majored in psychology in college and has volunteered in a number of mental health organizations. As a full-time researcher at the National Institute of Mental Health, she studies the disorders that children carry into adulthood, such as dyslexia, hyperactivity, and autism. She enjoys her work, but the FACT crisis hotline, where she counsels both abused children and child abusers, gives her an opportunity to deal with "a social problem as opposed to really more biologically-based problems."

The work is demanding, and Ashley had to go through an extensive training program before she could begin taking calls on her own. At one point she burned out, working thirty hours a month when the program was short of volunteers. And, there are those calls that are particularly demanding. Ashley admits that it's difficult talking to parents who have called to confess that they have just abused their children. But for Ashley, it's all a matter of perspective. "The bottom line is, you might not like this person that you're talking to, but it's important to think about the child, because when you hang up, what you say or what you've done to give this person some help, is really helping that child."

Despite the difficulty however, Ashley feels good about her efforts. "A lot of my friends say that volunteering is a selfless thing. But it's interesting, because I really enjoy the satisfaction that I get out of it. It's a really rewarding experience. That's enough to keep me going."

for foster parents, recreational programs for their children, and a crisis hotline and training programs for parents. Volunteers with counseling or medical backgrounds are sorely needed for these types of programs.

Crisis Hotlines

Hotlines give parents under stress a place to call for support and referral information. Hotline volunteers are trained to assist the parents in getting help for the problems that cause them to be violent or abusive toward their children. These programs usually have intensive training programs for which no previous counseling background is required.

Outreach Programs

Outreach programs are designed to keep the troubled family intact. Programs run by children's hospitals, community organizations, or national groups like Catholic Charities or NCPCA, pair volunteers with parents who have abusive tendencies. By visiting the troubled home on a regular basis, the volunteers support parents and reassure children.

In San Diego, the Parent Aid Prevention Program of the Children's Hospital and Health Center uses volunteers to make weekly telephone calls to abusive or high-risk families. The hospital's Child Advocate Program matches volunteers with incest victims for support and friendship. Other programs, such as Big Brothers/Sisters and Foster Grandparents, provide outside support to the children of troubled families.

Shelters and Foster Homes

Abused children working at emergency foster shelters, children's hospitals or shelters for battered families or runaway teenagers, volunteers can help children begin to heal the emotional wounds they have suffered from years of abuse. Ulrich Children's Home in Chicago, for instance, uses volunteers as baseball coaches, dance instructors, tutors and mentors. In these capacities, volunteers can help, either one-on-one or in a group setting, the children recover from their traumatic experiences by showing love and emotional support.

Children of Incarcerated Parents

With the increase in the number of single parent households, more and more children are finding their way into CPS agencies when their sole parent goes to prison. To provide a secure environment for these children and to maintain the relationship between parent and child during the incarceration, special programs have been created. One such program, Provident House, was the recipient of the 1990 President's Volunteer Action Award. Located in New Rochelle, New York, Provident House provides shelter, counseling and education to the children. It also provides frequent opportunities for the children to visit their incarcerated parents. Run by Catholic nuns, the program utilizes over one hundred volunteers as mentors, tutors, and social workers.

Advocacy

Voluntary organizations like NCPCA and other local groups that speak out for the welfare of children need volunteers to help lobby and educate the public on the problems of child abuse. Writers, office workers, lawyers, and other skilled people are needed to support the efforts of these organizations.

HELPING THE CHILDREN

Child abuse is a serious problem that is on the rise across the country. Millions of children are being denied the right to a safe and emotionally healthy childhood. The abused children who survive their abuse will grow up scarred and emotionally damaged. Many will pass on the cycle of abuse to the next generation. Volunteers are needed to help the overwhelmed child protective services system combat abuse. If you are motivated to help, contact your local clearinghouse or chapter of the NCPCA for information on volunteer needs.

CHAPTER NINE

Poverty In America

DAVID WATCHES and listens intently, his eyes closely following the math problem his teacher writes out on the blackboard. When she asks the third-grade class for the solution, David quickly raises his hand, sure of the answer. An avid reader with an immense curiosity, he enjoys the challenge of school and is among the class' brightest students.

But at home David's mood is much less confident and exuberant. At a time when he should be learning, growing, and having fun, his life is filled with fear and uncertainty. He is concerned about the growing number of drug dealers and street gang members living in his housing project. And after witnessing several shootings and beatings in his neighborhood, David is even fearful of walking to the corner grocery store.

And while the constant threat of violence is terrifying, David's greatest fears are hunger and the cold. The heater in his family's dilapidated apartment building breaks down far too often, while the meager welfare check they live on, $600 a month for a family of four, can't keep food in the house past the third week of the month.

David's teachers continue to try to encourage him. They tell him one day he will go on to college and become a successful lawyer. David wants to believe them, but reality tells him a different story. Most of the men in his housing project are unemployed; most have never gone to college; many never even completed high school. But for now, David will hold on to his dream of becoming a lawyer, despite the hopeless reality that is all around him.

AMERICA'S POOR

David's situation is not unique. One out of every five children in America lives in poverty. During the 1980s, the total number of people living in poverty in America increased by seven million, bringing the total to thirty-two million. The United States has the second highest poverty rate of any industrialized nation.

In America, poverty does not discriminate on the basis of race, sex or community. According to the 1988 census, 20.8 million of those in poverty were white, 9.4 million were black, while the remainder were Hispanic and other races. The majority of the nation's poor reside in small towns or rural communities; many others reside in middle-income urban and suburban neighborhoods. The remainder live in urban ghetto neighborhoods.

The nation's urban ghetto poor are the worst off. They not only experience the common problems of poverty, such as hunger and living in sub-standard housing, but they also face frightening levels of unemployment and violent crime. The ghetto poor live in socially and economically isolated areas of high-poverty; neighborhoods where welfare-dependency, illiteracy, poor health, and a lack of equal opportunity have become a way of life. With very few avenues for advancement, many of the urban ghetto poor remain indigent for generations.

WHO MAKES UP THE POOR

America's poor come from all walks of life. They are the working poor and those who receive welfare and unemployment benefits. They are two-parent families, single parents, single adults and children. They are white, black, Hispanic, and Asian. The largest single grouping of poor Americans, however, is single-parent families headed by females.

Single-Parent Families

According to the 1980 census, 25% of the families living below the poverty level were headed by white females, while over 58% were headed by black females. The causes are numerous: the soaring divorce rate; teen pregnancies; illegitimate births; and the high rate of incarceration, unemployment and death among minority males.

The nation's soaring divorce rate, which has tripled over the last twenty-five years, has contributed greatly to the increase in the number of poverty-level families that are headed by females.

One study showed that while the average husband's standard of living increases by 42% after divorce, that of the ex-wife drops a staggering 73%. With little to support herself and her children, divorced mothers are forced to fall back on welfare and public assistance.

Teen pregnancy and illegitimate births also play a large role. According to one study, one in ten women becomes pregnant before she reaches the age of twenty. Most of these children are born out of wedlock to men who are unable or unwilling to support them. Ironically, many women choose not to marry because the public aid programs favor single-parent households. Undereducated or unable to afford day-care for their children while they work, these mothers are effectively trapped in welfare, a dependency which in turn is passed on to their children. One study found that two-thirds of the daughters of mothers on welfare ended up on welfare themselves.

America's Youth

Since 1970, the percentage of the poor in this country that are children or teenagers has increased from 15% to 20%. These young people face a host of social problems. Each day in this country:

- 2,753 teenagers get pregnant
- 1,099 teenagers have abortions
- 1,287 teenagers give birth
- 367 teenagers miscarry
- 2,269 illegitimate babies are born
- 72 babies die before reaching one month of age
- 110 babies die before reaching one year of age
- 609 teenagers get gonorrhea or syphilis
- 3,288 children run away from home
- 49,322 youths are living in correctional facilities
- 2,989 kids see their parents divorced

Of course, the above social problems also affect youths whose family incomes are above the poverty level, but most of them impact the poor at a much higher rate.

Additional factors that contribute to the large number of black, single-parent families are the high rates of unemployment, violent death, and incarceration of black males. These factors greatly reduce the number of black men who are eligible for marriage. Young black men are dying at an incredible rate. The Federal Center for Disease Control claims that black males were safer doing active duty in the Vietnam War than residing in high-poverty neighborhoods. The Center's research shows that the homicide rate for black males between the ages of fifteen and twenty-four is ten times the rate for white males of the same age group.

The rates of incarceration and unemployment for black men are also astounding. According to Bureau of Justice statistics, black men comprise 46% of state prison inmates. And a 1989 Cook County (Chicago) study found that 29% of black males between the ages of twenty and twenty-nine had spent time in Cook County jail sometime during the year. This, combined with an unemployment rate for young black males approaching 30%, has greatly reduced the availability of black men to form two-parent families.

THE IMPACT OF POVERTY

Poverty is not an isolated problem. Its effects are broad and widespread, and it contributes greatly to many of our most pressing social ailments. Among these are:

Infant Mortality

In central Harlem, twenty-three out of every 1,000 babies die before their first birthday. One would have to look at Third World countries such as Malaysia to find such a high rate of infant death. Indeed, while the national average is ten deaths per 1,000 live births, in most impoverished neighborhoods the rate is at least twice that.

One of the primary causes of the high rate of infant mortality among the poor is the mother's inability to afford prenatal health care. A second cause, especially among teen parents, is a lack of knowledge about prenatal or infant care.

Malnutrition

An estimated twelve million children live in hunger in this country, a situation that results in stunted growth, learning disabilities, muscle weakness, vision problems, and even death. In Chicago alone, two or more children die daily from the effects of malnutrition. The Greater Chicago Food Depository also reported that another ten die weekly due to inadequate maternal nutrition. The parents are also negatively impacted. A malnourished mother is three times more likely to die during childbirth than one who receives adequate nutrition.

Homelessness

An estimated 30% of the country's homeless are families, while children that are homeless number as high as 750,000. Those who do have a place to live spend as much as 75% of their meager incomes on housing. Due to the high cost of housing, many poor families have doubled and tripled up in single apartments, where they are one domestic quarrel away from homelessness.

Lack of Education

Many low-income neighborhoods have high school drop-out rates well above the national average, exceeding 50% in some cases. This, combined with the high rate of illiteracy in these neighborhoods, leaves many poor lacking the basic educational tools necessary to work their way out poverty. Ineffective school systems, poor health, lack of positive role models and disruptive neighborhood environments all contribute to the lack of educational achievement.

Child Abuse

Children from families with annual incomes of less than $15,000 are five times more likely to be abused than children from higher-income families. Experts attribute this higher incidence of abuse among the poor to severe financial pressures, overcrowded living conditions, lack of parental experience and training, and the emotional stresses associated with being indigent.

ADDRESSING POVERTY IN AMERICA

The problem of poverty is the most complex social situation we face in America today. Although the core issue is inadequate income levels, other social concerns also play a major role in the poverty dilemma, such as the lack of job and educational opportunities, the increase in single parent families, and even racism.

For decades, public policy experts have intensely debated what can or should be done about the plight of the poor. Sociologist Charles Murray, a favorite among conservative politicians, argues that entitlement programs for the poor are ineffective. He feels that these programs actually help create the problems of poverty by reducing poor people's incentive to work and by reducing their self-esteem. In his book, *Losing Ground*, Murray offers the following alternative:

> The proposed program, our final and most ambitious thought experiment, consists of scrapping the entire federal welfare and income-support structure for working-aged persons, including AFDC, Medicaid, Food Stamps, Unemployment Insurance, Worker's Compensation, subsidized housing, disability insurance, and the rest.

While Murray's proposal sound's ludicrous, it was the direction policy-makers took in the 1980s; federal funding for entitlement programs, education, health and other social services was reduced substantially. The result, of course, was a dramatic increase in the number of poor, homeless, illiterate, and malnourished children.

Murray's contention that social programs are ineffective is refuted in a recent study by the Ford Foundation's Task Force on Social Welfare and the American Future. The Ford Foundation researchers found that Social Security, for instance, has cut the poverty rate among the elderly in half, while federally funded health centers have helped decrease the rate of infant mortality. The researchers also found that early childhood intervention programs, such as Headstart, have been extremely successful in increasing the odds for success for high-risk children. The study concludes that, "Social programs have been more successful than most Americans believe."

Recently, the Bush administration's public-policy experts took a fresh new look at ways to solve the problem of poverty. A White House task force on poverty recommended several new solutions to President Bush in July of 1990. The task force's proposals included expanding family planning services; giving tax credits to the working poor; providing block grants for programs that help poor children; instituting minimum child-support benefit levels; and establishing greater uniformity in eligibility requirements for food stamps, energy assistance, and welfare benefits. Unfortunately, these proposals were rejected by the White House due to lack of funds to pay for the new programs.

Hopefully, those in government will give these and similar recommendations for fighting poverty a second look. In the meantime, volunteers, national and community non-profit organizations, churches and schools will continue to lead the fight to help the nation's poor.

VOLUNTEERING TO HELP THE POOR

Many volunteer programs designed to combat individual social problems such as homelessness, illiteracy, and hunger benefit the poor, who are most often their victims. Other community-based programs, however, provide broad-based support to help the poor improve their overall living conditions and break out of the cycle of poverty. Many of these programs, which are run by community organizations, neighborhood churches, and other voluntary organizations, use volunteers to help impart much needed motivation, training, and guidance.

Community Organizations

Located in the heart of the inner-cities, these organizations provide a host of important services to the poor within their own communities. Funded by government, corporate and private grants, the programs and services of these organizations are tailored to the specific needs of their particular area. They address problems such as drug and alcohol abuse, housing shortages, crime prevention, prenatal care, and early childhood development. They also offer family counseling, job training and motivational programs.

In Milwaukee, a number of community organizations are working together to improve the living conditions within the city's economically depressed Westside. The Westside Neighborhood Service Center offers adult basic education and GED programs, elderly companion services, food and clothing banks, a Headstart program, assistance for victims of crime, and youth

Jobs for Youth

A model for other job training programs, Jobs for Youth utilizes over two hundred volunteers to provide educational and employment assistance to low-income youth in Chicago. The programs offered by Jobs for Youth include literacy training, job skill training, job placement and college preparatory classes.

A winner of the Presidential Volunteer Action Award, Jobs for Youth's performance record is impressive. Ninety percent of the young people who begin the job training program complete it. And through the agency's relationships with over 350 Chicago area businesses, 70% of the program's graduates have been able to secure employment.

The volunteer program at Jobs for Youth is also unique. It was designed for busy professionals and others who work in Chicago's business district. Jobs for Youth's employment training program is divided into one hour workshops, which allows volunteers to serve just one hour at a time. Consequently, volunteers can take an early or late lunch and lead an employment workshop. Volunteers who work at businesses supportive of Jobs for Youth's programs, such as First National Bank of Chicago, can take an hour out of the business day to volunteer.

Through Nicole Chaput, Jobs for Youth's volunteer director, volunteers receive a host of perks. Nicole regularly schedules events so that the agency's volunteers can meet their peers. Recent events not only included a volunteer recognition breakfast, but group outings at a ball game and the Chicago Blues Festival. In addition, Nicole and her staff put out a volunteer newsletter that provides information on current developments at Jobs for Youth, on new volunteers, and other "networking information."

Jobs for Youth is making a difference in the lives of low-income youth in Chicago while at the same time providing a comfortable, fulfilling, and fun environment for volunteers who want to help.

diversion programs to reduce the influence of gangs and drugs on teenagers. In addition, the Westside Community Development Corporation offers technical assistance and support to small businesses that provide jobs to neighborhood residents. The Westside Conservation Corporation runs housing programs to foster neighborhood rehabilitation and stabilization.

In New Orleans, both the Peoples Community Center and Saint Mark's Community Center offer day-care and learning programs for children of working mothers, recreation and youth development programs, and tutoring. On Philadelphia's southwest side, two organizations, the Southwest Frankford Community Center and the Southwest Human Services Project, provide educational programs, emergency assistance, youth recreational and diversion programs, and counseling to the area's needy residents.

Across the country, these organizations are making the biggest difference within inner-city communities. They need the help of volunteers with all types of backgrounds, both from in and outside of the community. People with business skills can assist in neighborhood economic development and housing programs. Teachers, medical professionals, and counselors can work in family counseling, as well as in educational and prenatal health programs. People who want to pursue their hobbies while volunteering can work in various youth recreational and diversion programs.

Church Programs

Neighborhood churches have long been a stabilizing force in low-income neighborhoods. Besides providing spiritual motivation and giving hope to their neighborhoods' downtrodden residents, many offer support services such as day-care, food and clothing banks, pre-school educational programs, and youth recreational programs.

Many churches from more upscale neighborhoods run tutoring and mentor programs for people in lower-income areas. In Chicago, two Gold Coast churches, Fourth Presbyterian and the LaSalle Street Church, match volunteers with adults and youths from the city's Cabrini Green housing project for tutoring and support. Another group of church volunteers, Fellowship of Friends, uses volunteers to rehabilitate vacant apartments in the Cabrini Green housing project.

Youth Development Program

One of the most important factors in breaking the cycle of poverty is to provide poverty-stricken children and youth with support, motivation and exposure to positive role models. By showing them how an education can help them lead more fulfilling lives, youth programs can encourage children and teens to stay in school and avoid crime and drugs.

National programs such as Boy Scouts, Girl Scouts, the YMCA, and the Boys Club use volunteers to teach leadership and life skills. Volunteers are needed for educational, camping and other recreational programs.

One-on-one programs use volunteers to lend personal support and guidance to disadvantaged youths. One national program, Big Brothers/Sisters, as well as many local programs, match volunteers with youths from single-parent or disadvantaged families.

In most urban areas, local voluntary organizations provide a host of services for the area's disadvantaged youth. In Cleveland, a number of youth programs and community centers, such as Collinwood Community Services Center, Coventry Youth Center, and the Community Youth Mediation Program, work to motivate and divert youths from crime, truancy, and drug use.

Neighborhood Health Clinics

In an effort to provide medical services to those who can't afford them, more and more free health clinics are being established in low-income neighborhoods. In Tampa, the Judeo-Christian Health Clinic's staff of volunteer doctors, dentists, optometrists, pharmacists, and laymen provide free health services to those without health insurance or public assistance. In Miami, the Camillus Health Concern uses over two hundred volunteers to provide health services to the indigent, while the Los Angeles Free Clinic's 450 volunteers provides medical services to over 30,000 patients a year.

Other Organizations

The National Urban League, founded to provide equal opportunities for the nation's minorities, offers many programs to improve the lives of the disadvantaged. Located in cities across the country, the Urban League uses volunteers in job training and counseling programs, illiteracy programs, family counseling, housing development, and emergency social service programs. Other national organizations, such as Catholic Charities, run centers in low-income communities that provide food and housing assistance, educational and vocational training programs, and family and teen pregnancy counseling.

In Miami, the Camillus Health Concern uses over two hundred volunteers to provide free medical services to thousands of

The Suburban Poor

While most of the attention given to the poverty-stricken focuses on the homeless or those living in inner-city slums, a recent study centers on a "new" group of poor, the suburban poor. Suburban communities, like those located on the borders of such cities as Chicago, Los Angeles, St. Louis, and Philadelphia, house 9.5 million indigent, many with incomes lower than their peers in inner-city, low-income housing projects. In fact, Chicago held the dubious distinction of having both the richest and poorest suburbs in the country, Kenilworth with a per capita income of $61,950, and Ford Heights, at $4,943.

The suburban poor in many ways are worse off than their inner-city counterparts. While having most of the problems of the inner-cities, such as drugs, high unemployment rates, and violent crimes, they lack the cities' commercial tax bases to fund social services and police protection. They have little public transportation to connect them to job opportunities in other areas.

While the majority of the suburban poor are white Americans, the percentage of blacks and Hispanics, currently 25% and 22% of this poor population respectively, has been increasing. Once a place to which minorities fled the inner-cities for a better life, many of these suburbs have all but become rural ghettos.

indigent patients annually. At public housing projects across the country, resident and nonresident volunteers are banding together to rehab their homes and save their children from the effects of drugs and street gangs.

HELPING THE INNER-CITY POOR

Across the country, there are run-down urban neighborhoods and rural communities filled with indigent adults and children. By working with local community centers, churches, youth programs or with select national organizations, volunteers can help poverty-stricken persons improve their circumstances. If you are concerned about the poor in your city, contact your volunteer clearinghouse for information on the hundreds of ways that you can make a difference.

CHAPTER TEN

Teens In Crisis

EW ADULTS can truly appreciate the real pressures that are part of the daily lives of teenagers today. Many parents have forgotten the anxiety they themselves felt as teens—the social pressure to conform and fit in, the confusion associated with a maturing sexuality, the intimidation and harassment of older kids. High school has also changed a lot since most parents were students. Drugs — hard drugs like heroin, crack, PCP — can be bought easily in the hallways, sexual activity is more common, and gangs are a visible part of many schools. The pressure to do well academically and get into top-ranked colleges has also increased tremendously. Contemporary problems facing the once stable family—both parents working outside the home, divorce, separation—make being a teenager even more difficult.

With so much pressure confronting teenagers, it's not surprising that more and more of them are running away from home, dropping out of school, turning to drugs, or attempting suicide. And this does not just apply to teenagers who are the products of broken homes, poverty, or child abuse. Teens in crisis come from a wide range of financial and sociological backgrounds, and their numbers are growing every year.

THE PROBLEMS

Runaways

This year alone, a reported one million American teenagers will run away from home. But the real number is probably much higher, since the majority of runaways goes unreported because parents are either not concerned enough to call the police or afraid of the information becoming public.

While most teens that run away return home, the ones who do not face a bleak future. They have to turn to the streets for their

117

livelihood with many of the females turning to prostitution and the boys resorting to theft and other crimes to survive. They also become victims of the streets. The incidence of sexual assault, drug use and criminal arrest among runaways is well above that of other teens.

Teen Pregnancy

The teen pregnancy rate in the United States is the highest of any developed nation: nearly one million teenage girls get pregnant every year in this country. Almost one in ten will become

---

The Metrohelp Hotline: "A Cold Slap Of Reality"

Sandra Gaines is the Research Coordinator at Metrohelp, one of four national runaway hotline services. It is run by a small core of employees and a large staff of part-time volunteers whose primary goal, according to Gaines, "is to assist the youth in crisis."

Kids can call Metrohelp's 800 number for assistance at any time from anywhere in the country. Volunteers use a directory which lists over 7,000 agencies nationwide to refer callers to shelters, Traveller's Aid locations, free transportation, crisis intervention centers, self-help groups, and job banks, to name a few.

Metrohelp also takes and relays messages between runaways and their parents. Perhaps as a result, parents frequently call, not only to inquire about missing children or to relay messages, but also to talk about their own problems. Metrohelp volunteers work with them as much as possible and refer them to other related organizations when necessary. But as one volunteer said, the role of the parent in most runaway cases is too vital to have them quickly referred to another agency.

Teens use the hotline for help with an assortment of problems, from academic pressures to severe drug abuse. One common characteristic Gaines sees in all the callers, however, is a tendency to fantasize about what it would be like to be away from home. "They don't realize the difficulty of supporting and defending yourself on the streets." As a result, Metrohelp tries to give them an idea of what it would be like to be out on your own. Or as Gaines puts it, to give fantasizing teens thinking about running away a "cold slap of reality."

pregnant before they reach the age of twenty. And a large majority of these women are not even in their late teens; more and more of them are girls younger than fifteen years old. Indeed, the number of girls who become pregnant before their fifteenth birthday has tripled during the past decade.

In the last twenty years, teenage women have become more sexually active; nearly half of the female population between the ages of fourteen and twenty claims to have had sexual intercourse. Although the use of birth control has increased (70% of all sexually active girls use some type of birth control), the United States still has the lowest rate of contraceptive use among sexually active teenagers. As a result more teens have become pregnant, and a greater number are turning to abortion to rid themselves of unwanted babies. According to one study, sixty out of 1,000 teenagers will have an abortion by the age of eighteen.

Drug and Alcohol Abuse

Our nation's drug problem, especially among the youth, has long been the focus of unprecedented national concern. A look at the statistics justifies these concerns: a reported 60% of high school seniors in America have used drugs, and one-third of all twelve to seventeen year olds have been or are regular drinkers. One out of every six American children has tried marijuana, while one in every three has tried alcohol before reaching ninth grade.

Two of the most dangerous and addictive drugs, cocaine and its by-product, crack, are quickly becoming more widespread. Crack use may pose the most serious problem because it accelerates all the side effects of coke, including addiction. It has been shown that the first high on crack triggers an immediate craving for more. Lower-income youths are especially prone to crack addiction because of the drug's relatively low cost.

Yet alcohol is by far the most popular drug of choice for middle- and upper-class youths. According to a 1986 study, 65% of the high school seniors polled said they had used alcohol within the past month, as compared to 39% for marijuana and 6% for cocaine.

Drop-Outs

Every year nearly one million high school students drop out of school all together or are so chronically absent that they can't amass even the minimum number of attendance days required to graduate to the next grade. Although students from all types of communities across the country drop out of school, drop-out rates are highest among poor, inner-city students. In some urban areas, the drop-out rate exceeds 50%.

Suicide

Even to those who recognize teen suicide as a major issue, the statistics are still shocking: One out of every four teenagers has attempted suicide, which adds up to 400,000 attempts each year, or one almost every eighty seconds. Out of these attempts, nearly 5,000 are successful. The incidence of suicide among teenagers is eight times that of the general population. As a leading cause of death among adolescents, it ranks behind only accidents and homicide; for youths between fifteen and twenty-four, it ranks second behind death due to accidents.

VOLUNTEERING TO SAVE A GENERATION

A number of programs have been developed to meet the needs of troubled teenagers. National community-based organizations, such as Boy and Girl Scouts, Boys and Girls Clubs, and the YMCA/YWCA, run recreational, camping, and arts and crafts programs for all young adults. Local organizations, churches and schools have also developed programs to help today's youth cope. In addition to recreational and educational programs, these organizations also provide counseling, drug use prevention and rehabilitation programs, and pregnancy prevention programs.

The primary objective of these various programs is to provide teenagers with positive role models, good values, and healthy environments in which to expend energy in constructive ways. Although numerous, these programs can be divided into the following areas: hotlines, counseling and recreational programs, job-training programs, shelters, and specialty programs.

Hotlines

Hotlines are popular with teens because they offer teens a confidential and non-judgmental avenue to discuss their fears and concerns. Today, there are both national and local hotline services teens can access. These hotlines address concerns such as depression, drug abuse, family violence, sex-related problems, and running away, as well as suicide.

Most hotlines use volunteers to take incoming calls. It is not always an easy assignment. To be successful, the volunteer must be able to listen creatively to the caller. Through careful listening, the volunteer can hear the "real" problem through the confusion and panic of the caller. Once that is accomplished, the volunteer can help the caller see his or her situation more objectively, and then steer the caller to the appropriate counseling service, shelter, clinic or other resource.

Counseling and Recreational Programs

The most common way of providing assistance to youths, these programs offer a number of services, including counseling groups for drug/alcohol abuse, sexuality, or family strife; tutoring and educational programs; teen pregnancy groups; and recreational activities. Programs for Teens, which is run by the Silver Spring Neighborhood Center in Milwaukee, provides teens from a local housing project with both recreational activities and educational programs. Among the many services it offers are rap groups, an alternative school, and summer employment. A sim-

How Helpful Are Hotlines?

A 1988 study by Gingerich, Gurney and Wirtz on "How Helpful are Hotlines?" indicates that hotlines are making a difference. In the survey of hotline callers, nine out of ten people polled said they had been helped by the service. About half of these felt their problem seemed less severe after talking with a counselor during a follow-up call than it had been when they first called.

From "How Helpful Are Hotlines? A Survey of Callers," Wallace Gingerich, Raymond Gurney, and Thomas Wirtz, *Social Casework*, December 1988.

ilar program in Chicago, Youth Service Project, has additional programs for pregnant teens, youths involved in gangs, and high school drop-outs who want to pass the GED exam.

National programs, such the Boys and Girls Clubs of America, the Boy and Girl Scouts, and the YMCA/YWCA, offer teens an endless number of recreational, educational, and crisis support programs. Volunteer opportunities are also endless. Coaches and trainers are needed for swimming, baseball, soccer and many other sports. People are also needed to teach photography, woodworking, computer skills, dance and music. Other volunteer opportunities include leading camping trips, providing career guidance, and mentoring.

Job Training Programs

Teens who have dropped out of high school have little chance of securing a decent job unless they obtain a high school diploma equivalent and some job skills training. Programs like Jobs for Youth, a Chicago-based job skills training program, gives teens the second chance they need. By first offering GED, business and other job skills training, and then placing their students with cooperating employers, Jobs for Youth helps former drop-outs turn their lives around. Volunteers are needed for all phases of the program, including leading workshops and teaching college preparation classes.

Shelters

Shelters provide emergency and longer-term housing for runaways and homeless youths. In addition to housing, however, most shelters offer services related to teen problems, such as hotlines, peer counseling, and group counseling with the goal of family reunification. The Larkin Street Youth Center in San Francisco, for example, aims its services at reuniting teens with their families whenever possible. Counseling is provided, in addition to medical screenings and treatment, GED preparation, and social programs. San Francisco's Huckleberry House is also interested in family reunification. It runs a crisis hotline and offers family counseling and transportation back to legal guardians when needed.

Outreach Programs

To reach runaway teens, a number of programs have been developed in which volunteers go out into the street to persuade

---

TRAINING FOR TEEN CRISIS VOLUNTEERS

Training for teen crisis volunteers usually includes an initial orientation program, in which the agency's philosophy, mission, and services are explained. The training program also outlines general rules and guidelines, such as the limits of physical intervention and volunteer responsibility. Volunteers are also given basic instruction in administrative functions, such as how to use the phones and business equipment. Orientation programs are regularly scheduled and usually take a full day to complete. The program at San Francisco's Larkin Street Youth Center runs six hours. Following the training, volunteers are asked to make a commitment to the program, generally anywhere from two to six months for weekly shifts of three hours.

Volunteers are then given further training in their specific jobs. Tutors, drop-in counselors, and hotline operators are given separate training in their fields.

Hotline training programs vary according to each individual hotline service, but they do share some basic methods and goals. A typical program lasts from fifteen to forty hours, which is spread out in sessions over the course of one or two weeks. Through demonstration, small group discussion, and role playing, trainees learn how to listen creatively, handle typical and unusual situations, and separate themselves personally from a caller's problems. Volunteers are shown how to set limits on their involvement in order to avoid burnout. Trainees are also required to examine their own lives and prejudices, especially their reasons for volunteering, as well as their expectation of the work. As one instructor says, "It's a two-way street; you should get something out of it, too."

Trainees also learn what is not included in their job. They are not to give legal or medical advice; a back-up staff is responsible for that kind of information. This guarantees that callers are getting correct information and proper care, and it keeps legal matters and insurance requirements under control

Training usually ends with the trainee making a commitment, usually six months to a year. This is not a legal or written commitment, but it does stress the volunteer's importance within the organization.

teens to use the shelters and counseling services available to them. One program, Children of the Night, seeks to help exploited teen prostitutes in Hollywood, California turn their lives around. Similar programs across the country need volunteers willing to go out and talk to runaways, gang members, and drug addicted teens about seeking help.

Specialty Programs

There are a number of youth programs across the country that offer specific services, such as athletic activities, teen pregnancy programs, and youth advocacy (in which staff members and volunteers attend court with clients and talk with teachers on their behalf). San Diego's Adolescent and Parenting Program helps to care for pregnant youths. In a different type of program, Athletes for Youth helps Milwaukee County teenagers learn team values and the importance of teamwork. Volunteers in all capacities are needed for these programs.

BECOME A TEEN CRISIS VOLUNTEER

People of all types are needed to staff organizations catering to adolescents. There is no "ideal" volunteer, although many teenagers are naturally drawn to this area of service. Other valuable workers include retired people, young mothers, community newcomers, students of social work and psychology, college service clubs, and busy professionals wanting to give something back to the community.

As an individual volunteer, you may never know how much you are doing for your community. Most of your work will be in response to those who need your help, but few of those you help will come back to say "thanks, it worked." But the proliferation of youth services should assure you that your help is needed. As one volunteer says, "Life is not fair. It never was, it never will be. The point is to keep on helping." You may not solve the world's problems through volunteering, but you can help young, troubled individuals solve theirs.

There are many types of youth programs for different kinds of volunteers. You don't have to have experienced a problem like the one you're trying to help solve, nor do you have to be perfect yourself to give others advice. You just need concern, patience, and a commitment to helping young people help themselves. If you think this might be the area for you, contact your local hospital for more information. The hospitals usually keep listings of local hotlines and related services. To receive a copy of the National Directory of Hotlines write to the Program Coordinator at the National Youth Alternatives Project, 1830 Connecticut

TEENAGE VOLUNTEERS

One of the most exciting developments in volunteering has been the rapid increase in the number of teenagers joining the ranks of volunteers. From college campuses to high schools throughout America, teenagers are pitching in to help people with disabilities, the poor, the elderly and their fellow teens.

More and more high schools are starting service organizations that promote peer counseling and community service. Peer counseling programs allow teen volunteers to assist their fellow classmates with academic, social or family problems. In addition, the teens get involved in service projects outside of school. For instance, students at Suitland High School in Maryland visit a local nursing home once a week, tutor at-risk elementary students three times a week, and work with adults with disabilities at the Capitol Concept Center. Other examples are the R.E.A.C.H. program in Nebraska, in which high school students teach elementary students about the dangers of drug abuse, and the Independent Aging Program's Intergenerational Project in Santa Clara, California, in which high school and college students assist area seniors with yard work, grocery shopping, and other errands.

But the largest growth in teen volunteering has occurred on college campuses. The Campus Outreach Opportunity League, C.O.O.L., assists students on over 300 college campuses in getting involved in helping their communities. At the University of Illinois, the Volunteer Illini Project, the largest student-run volunteer campaign in the country, numbers over 1,000 students, who work with the disabled, elderly, illiterate and poor in their community.

For teens, volunteer opportunities abound. From high school to college to community-based programs, young people of all ages can lend a hand—and in return, receive the joys that come from service.

Avenue, N.W., Washington, D.C. 20009. Another resource is your local chapter of the National Alliance of Information and Referral Services.

CHAPTER ELEVEN

Illiteracy

THE FIRST THING Alice does when she comes into her third period high school English class is lay her head down on top of her desk and fall asleep. By the fourth week of school she is already well behind in her work, and when the final exam is given at the end of the semester, she doesn't even bother to show up. But Alice is not failing tenth-grade English because she is too tired to stay awake. The reason is much more basic than that: Alice can't read, and to hide that embarrassing fact from her teacher and friends, she pretends to be asleep.

Unlike Alice, Charles never made it to the tenth grade. Raised on public aid, he dropped out of school when he was twelve to help support his mother and two sisters. His mother, who was illiterate, never pushed Charles to study or to attend class. As a result, his reading ability never progressed beyond the second-grade level.

Despite his illiteracy, Charles was able to rise to the level of foreman at work. He enjoys his job, but he lives in fear that his co-workers and friends will find out that he can't read. Now age fifty-two, Charles says he is determined that his grandchildren will know the importance of a good education. Enrolled in a literacy program across town, Charles looks forward to the day he can read a book to his two granddaughters.

Charles and Alice are just two of the estimated twenty-seven million Americans who are considered functionally illiterate by the U.S. Department of Education. Alice is one of the many students our educational system has crippled by passing them from grade to grade with their peers even though they have never learned to read, solve rudimentary problems, or perform simple mathematical functions. Charles was one of the estimated one million students who drop out of the nation's school systems each year. Together with the millions of immigrants who can hardly speak English at all, drop-outs like Charles, as well as those still enrolled like Alice, comprise a large part of the nation's illiterate population.

Illiterates lack the basic reading and writing skills that are needed to function adequately in society. While some of them read at a fifth-grade level or lower, most cannot read at all. As a consequence, illiterates are unable to perform the most common and necessary tasks the majority of us take for granted—reading a newspaper, shopping at a grocery store, ordering from a menu, applying for a job. They can't read street signs, cereal boxes, warning labels, or even their paychecks. In short, they can't fully participate in everyday life.

WHO ARE THE ILLITERATE?

Illiteracy cuts across all social and economic levels. With over twenty million people, white adults make up the largest group of illiterate Americans. But it is Hispanic and black adults, those who have traditionally been denied access to high-quality education and whose cultures often don't emphasize learning English or reading, that have the highest *rates* of illiteracy. Fifty-six percent of adult Hispanics are functionally illiterate in English, a staggering number but one muted by the fact that English is frequently the second language for many Hispanics. Blacks follow closely behind with a 44% illiteracy rate. Sixteen percent of whites can't read.

As with race, illiteracy is not confined to any one age group. While the greatest number of illiterates are found in the elderly population, young adults from eighteen to twenty-nine years old who can't read also make up a sizeable group. And while many of us think the problem is confined to large inner-cities, where poverty, homelessness, drug abuse, and gang warfare are more common, the fact is that over 50% of illiterates live in small towns and suburbs. Studies are beginning to show that illiteracy is indeed a *national* problem, and one that is much more widespread than originally thought.

THE CAUSES

The causes of illiteracy, as is true of most social ills, are various and complex. Factors such as poverty, malnutrition, learning disabilities, and unstable family situations contribute greatly to the problem, as do the illiteracy of parents, lack of motivation, and emotional problems.

The school systems share part of the blame. Large class sizes and a lack of classroom discipline make it difficult for first- and second-grade teachers to give slower or unmotivated students the individualized attention they need to acquire reading skills. Unable to read at this critical point, these students are either lost in the shuffle by overworked teachers or are allowed to graduate

Profile of Illiteracy

A University of Texas study, using the Adult Performance Level measurement commissioned by the U.S. Department of Education, estimates that over thirty-three million people are functionally illiterate. Based on the 1980 Census, the demographic breakdown of the segment of the population that is illiterate is as follows:

ILLITERACY BY SEX	% Illiterate	Total Number
Females over 18	23%	20,056,000
Males over 18	17%	13,454,820
ILLITERACY BY RACE		
Hispanic over 18	56%	5,057,024
Black over 18	44%	7,793,280
White over 18	16%	23,154,880
ILLITERACY BY AGE		
60 years and older	35%	12,470,850
50-59 years	28%	6,530,440
40-49 years	19%	4,323,640
30-39 years	11%	3,467,310
18-29 years	16%	7,887,200

Used by permission. Coalition for Literacy, *Fact Sheet: Adult Literacy in the United States.*

in order to keep them with their peers. Even if their illiteracy is discovered in junior or senior high, students who can't read are then confronted by schools which, underfunded and under-staffed, don't have the programs designed to help them. Dis-couraged and unable to do high school work, these students flunk or drop out, compelled to work at low-level service jobs for the rest of their lives. Those who manage to hide their illiteracy or who are nevertheless graduated by teachers who are aware of it, are handed high school diplomas they can't read.

Social problems such as poverty and crime negatively impact a student's ability to learn. Some children living in poverty suffer from poor health due to inadequate diets, some even suffer from malnutrition. This hampers their ability to concentrate and learn. In high-crime areas, violence in the schools diverts a student's attention from his or her studies. Street gangs forcefully recruit children as young as ten years old to boost gang membership and to peddle drugs in the schoolyard. During the 1984-85 school year, the Detroit Public School System registered 228 shootings and twenty-five fatalities.

Unstable family situations also impair a student's ability to learn. Students from dysfunctional homes, those that are either violent or have alcoholic or negligent parents, find it difficult to complete homework assignments or concentrate in school because of emotional stress.

Other students suffer from learning disabilities. Students with these problems are often incorrectly classified as slow learn-ers, and are frequently given up on. A hearing aid, eyeglasses, or even the recognition of the existence of a learning disability or emotional problem could have been the answer to these students' slow learning and resulting illiteracy.

The problem of illiteracy is especially acute in Hispanic com-munities. Having recently come to America and unable to speak English, immigrants from Mexico, Cuba, and other Spanish-speaking countries settle in ethnic enclaves in which English is rarely spoken. Children raised in this environment learn to speak Spanish as their primary language, often either never learning English at all or learning it poorly as a second language. This problem is bound to increase as more and more Hispanics settle in the United States.

THE COST OF ILLITERACY

Whatever the reasons, the price of illiteracy for the person who cannot read is beyond calculation. But the problem is by no means just an individual one—it extends to all of us. Illiteracy is at the root of many social and economic problems. The Working

---

Close, Yet So Far

One of the most majestic structures in downtown Chicago, the white gothic brick steeple of the Fourth Presbyterian Church rises high above Michigan Avenue. Located on Chicago's "Magnificent Mile," Fourth Presbyterian sits among the expensive high-rise condominiums and up-scale stores frequented by the city's upper-income residents.

Less than two miles directly west, the stark, worn high rises of a public housing project loom above the run-down tenements in an area called Cabrini Green. The boarded and burned-out windows of many of the apartments there seem to visually confirm the misery and the discontent of its residents. The neighborhood, considered by many to be the worst in Chicago, is notorious for its abject poverty and high crime rate.

Geographically close but economically worlds apart, Fourth Presbyterian Church and Cabrini Green do have something in common: the church tutoring program. Since 1963, members of Fourth Presbyterian have volunteered to tutor disadvantaged children from Cabrini Green in basic reading, writing, and math.

Working one-on-one with the children, the volunteers usually develop a "Big Brother/Big Sister" attachment with their students. Many of the volunteers go beyond their weekly ninety-minute tutoring sessions to help these deprived children develop a healthy sense of self-esteem and a will to learn.

The Fourth Presbyterian Tutor Program is an example of the efforts being made by churches and community organizations across the country to combat illiteracy. In doing so, they not only help the students learn reading skills, but they also help them realize that there is a world outside their depressing surroundings. And by educating and motivating these students, the volunteers get them closer to becoming a part of that world.

Group of Adult Literacy, a coalition of eleven educational groups, points to the clear connection between illiteracy and other issues, such as welfare dependency, underdeveloped parenting skills, crime, and decreased productivity. Barbara Bush, acknowledging this point, in a recent interview said, "I believe if we can lick the problem of people being functionally illiterate, we will then go on to solve most of the other major problems besetting this country."

In terms of lost productivity, lower tax revenues, welfare, crime, and other connected problems, the cost of illiteracy to the country is truly staggering. The chairman of B. Dalton Booksellers, which is currently running its own literacy campaign, estimates that illiteracy is costing the country $225 billion a year. And as our economy moves from a manufacturing base to a service-oriented one in which a higher rate of literacy is required for entry-level positions, the cost will be even higher. The initial effects are already visible. When New York Telephone recently looked to fill openings for operators and repairmen, only 14% of the 22,880 applicants passed the qualifying test.

Illiteracy perpetuates a self-defeating cycle of unemployment, poverty, and crime. Parents who cannot read often pass illiteracy down to their children, enslaving them to either similar low-paying service jobs or unemployment and poverty. The Labor Department and other groups have well documented the strong correlation between a low level of education and a high rate of unemployment. With little hope of getting ahead financially or socially, many illiterates turn to crime. According to the Correctional Association, 60% of the jail population across the country can't read above a third-grade level. And there is no way of determining what sort of marginal lives illiteracy has forced others into, but no doubt a significant number of such groups as the homeless, runaway teens, and prostitutes don't know how to read. These problems seem so far removed from us, but all of us are affected by them in one way or another.

ILLITERACY IN THE WORKPLACE

In this high-paced economic age, companies are fighting to survive in the face of increased foreign and domestic competition, the high cost of doing business, and the constant threat of takeovers and mergers. To gain that needed economic edge, businesses are forced to run leaner and meaner, and to do so they need workers who can quickly assimilate new information, work with new technology, and hit the ground running.

Knowing this, businesses are looking at their workforces with concern, and for good reason. Some forty-five million of their employees are either functionally illiterate or barely literate, 30% of which are unskilled workers, 29% semi-skilled workers, and 11% professionals (including managers and technicians). Illiteracy is costing business more than $20 billion a year. As if they didn't already have their hands full with these workers, companies will have to deal with the 2.3 million new functional illiterates who join the workforce every year.

SOCIAL POLICY TO COMBAT ILLITERACY
The Federal Government

Recently, as literacy has gained a high political profile and as the staggering cost of illiteracy has become better known, government, business, and organizations in the private sector have been redoubling their efforts to combat the problem. The federal government funnels nearly $300 million a year into literacy programs through its various educational programs, of which the Adult Education Program is one of the largest. Administered by the state, the program provides basic instruction in literacy and English as a second language to adults who are functionally illiterate. The government also funds the literacy efforts of such groups as the VISTA Literacy Corps, the Job Corps, and the Job Training Partnerships Act. Recruits in the armed forces who have a low level of literacy are given remedial reading courses in order to bring them up to a ninth-grade reading level.

Local Government

The primary thrust of local governments in combatting illiteracy is in improving and expanding their school systems. In Chicago, whose school system was described by former Secretary of Education William Bennet as "the worst in the nation," major reforms are underway to raise the reading levels of its students. The plan includes increasing parental involvement, raising the quality of the teaching staff, and using more volunteers as tutors, counseling assistants, and teacher's aides. Many other school systems, such as New York City's, also make use of volunteers, freeing teachers so that they can spend more time actually teaching.

Many cities across the country are combatting illiteracy through their public libraries. The Library Literary Program of the Federal Office of Education Research Information funds state and local libraries to run and coordinate literacy programs. Staffed mainly by volunteers, these libraries offer classes and tutoring in basic reading and writing.

The Corporate Sector

Recognizing the high economic stakes involved, businesses are becoming actively involved in fighting illiteracy in the workplace. One-third of major U.S. corporations provide remedial courses in reading, writing, and arithmetic to their employees. McGraw-Hill and B. Dalton Booksellers, in particular, have taken the lead on this front. In 1983, Harold McGraw, chairman of the McGraw-Hill publishing house, founded the Business Council for Effective Literacy, a group of business leaders dedicated to eliminating illiteracy. B. Dalton has set aside $3 million for its own nationwide literacy campaign, which has enlisted the support of major corporations and is looking to recruit and train 50,000 volunteers. Initiatives by other businesses, such as Capital Cities/ABC, include advertising campaigns encouraging illiterates to seek help in learning how to read.

The Non-Profit Sector

Much of the battle against illiteracy is being waged by countless independent, not-for-profit groups across the country. Volunteers are used extensively. Among the largest national literacy groups using volunteers are Literacy Volunteers of America and Laubach Literacy, Inc.

Founded in Syracuse, New York, Literacy Volunteers was originally established to help the illiterate population in its hometown. Since then, however, the group has expanded to include programs in thirty-five states, where 27,000 trained volunteers provide free, individual instruction in basic literacy and English as a second language (ESL). With 98,000 trained volunteers,

Laubach Literacy is an even larger organization, providing similar instruction in literacy and ESL to more than 100,000 students annually. Through its press, Laubach Literacy publishes books and a newspaper directed at adult beginning readers. Both organizations have numerous local chapters throughout the country.

Despite the federal and state government allocations of more resources for literacy programs, as well as increasing numbers of volunteer tutors, the battle against illiteracy is far from being won. With the number of illiterate adults increasing by two million every year, much more needs to be done to substantially reduce the nation's illiterate population.

BECOMING A LITERACY TUTOR

Volunteers are one of the nation's most effective weapons against illiteracy. They can help by working in clerical positions in schools

Patience In Tutoring

"The kid didn't want to learn anything," explained Kathleen. "All she wanted me to do was take her to get ice cream." Kathleen, a tutor in a program for disadvantaged young adults, was expressing her frustration at her lack of progress with a new student. Fortunately, Kathleen persisted, and her student began to rapidly pick up new reading and writing skills.

Working with illiterate students, whether they are adults or children, requires patience. While the volunteer may want to achieve immediate results, the student is the one who determines the pace of progress.

In most cases, students are not illiterate because they lack intelligence, but because of reasons such as mistrust of teachers, fear of failure or ridicule, learning disabilities, or unstable family situations. Before they can begin to learn, they have to feel comfortable and "safe" with their tutors. Some students may even feel the need to test their tutors in order to assure themselves that their tutor really cares about them as individuals.

Tutoring in many cases is not just teaching. It is a one-on-one relationship with a person who has special needs. It is demanding work that requires the tutor to be not just a good teacher, but an understanding, creative, and patient one as well.

and literacy programs or by becoming literacy tutors.

Working one-on-one with a student allows a tutor to break through the barriers that have kept the student from learning in the past. Tutors can be especially effective in helping students overcome the fear of failure or ridicule, a lack of self-confidence or motivation, and feelings of helplessness. Helen H. Acker, founder of the New York City School Volunteer Program, has established her program on the belief that teachers have to first make their students *believe* they can learn before trying to teach them. Literacy volunteers can do just that.

As a tutor, you are challenged not only to teach, but also to motivate your student. Tutor and student often develop a friendship or a big brother/sister relationship. As a friend and tutor, the volunteer reaps the rewards that come from watching a student learn to read, and as a consequence, gain self-confidence and self-esteem.

The only qualifications that a literacy volunteer needs are the ability to read and write well and an interest in helping others do the same. To be an effective tutor, however, requires patience, dedication and enthusiasm. Volunteers should also be willing to allot a few hours a week to tutor, prepare lessons, and attend meetings and training sessions.

The prospective tutor has the choice of a number of programs through which to volunteer. In addition to the local branches of Literacy Volunteers of America and Laubach Literacy, local school systems and city libraries use literacy volunteers extensively. There are also programs offered by multi-purpose organizations, such as the YMCA and the Urban League, and by numerous church and community groups. Contact your local clearinghouse for a list of literacy programs needing volunteers.

Volunteer Training

After volunteers have signed up with a literacy program, they are usually required to attend a training program, which presents the most effective techniques for teaching illiterates how to read. Trainees are given instruction in developing a student's thinking and comprehension skills, planning lessons, and evaluating student progress. Since illiterate students will come

Sample Tutor Job Description

ADULT BASIC EDUCATION PROGRAM

Hours:

Supervisor:

Location:

Beginning date: _____ **Ending date:** _____

Skills required:
1. High school diploma or equivalent.
2. Patience to let student progress at own pace.
3. Ability to analyze student's strength and weakness.
4. Flexibility to adapt to student's acceptance of activity.
5. Creativity to eliminate repetition and boredom.

Training required:
1. Attend 30-minute orientation and observe tutor working with student.
2. Attend planning session with teacher prior to beginning assignment.

Goals and objectives:
1. Know student and student goals.
2. Provide student with positive feedback.
3. Make sure student accomplishes some task, whether large or small, before he/she leaves session.
4. Establish rapport with student to maintain a close relationship.

Job description:
1. Tutor works on one-on-one basis with student to help student learn and accomplish his/her goals.
2. Tutor works under direction of teacher even though sessions may be held in locations other than a classroom.
3. Assist student in charting goals and keeping a record of achievement.
4. Try to help student take responsibility for his/her learning.

From literacy manual, *Volunteers In Adult Basic Education.*

from a variety of backgrounds and age groups, the program encourages tutors to tailor the sessions to meet the individual needs of their students. The initial training course usually takes up to fifteen hours to complete, and subsequent programs are held during the following months.

After the training sessions, many literacy organizations require volunteers to make a six-month commitment to the program, which includes attending regular tutoring sessions, additional training programs, and meetings. A student's progress depends heavily on consistent instruction and encouragement, and a stable tutor-student relationship will help facilitate learning.

After completing the training course and committing to the program, volunteers are matched with students based on volunteer preferences (such as a student's age, literacy level, and gender) when possible. The tutoring sessions take place either once or twice a week for an hour or two, and are held at a location and time mutually convenient for both the student and the volunteer.

TEACHING SOMEONE TO READ

Teaching others to read is one of the most satisfying and positive volunteer experiences. The volunteers get direct feedback from their efforts as they watch their students learn to read and write. Even more satisfying is seeing the students' self-confidence build as they learn, because for the beginning reader the ability to read does not just open up the world of books, it opens up the world.

CHAPTER TWELVE

The Abandoned Elderly

MORE AND MORE, they seem to be everywhere you look: taking your order from behind the counters of McDonald's or Burger King, plugging everything from life insurance to Western Union telegrams on T.V. commercials, exchanging barbs and witticisms in movies and prime-time sitcoms. But these are not teenagers or the young stars we expect to see in these roles—they are the elderly, and they are quickly becoming the largest and most visible segment of our society.

Yet for every elderly face we see, there are thousands more outside our view in hospitals, nursing homes, retirement centers, and their own homes. And for many of these unseen elderly, their lives are not filled with the vibrant energy of the retired men and women in the television commercials or the laughter and fun family life of the elderly ladies on "The Golden Girls." No, these are the abandoned elderly, the ones who spend their days lonely and withdrawn, without any of the love, companionship, and help that make life worthwhile for all of us. To make their situation even worse, many of today's elderly are in dire financial straits, unable to afford needed medical treatment and drugs, housing, or the extended medical care of a declining spouse. It would surprise a number of us to know of the increasing rates of alcoholism, drug addiction, and suicide among the elderly population, but we would be less perplexed if we were to look closely at the difficult lives many of them lead. The plight of the elderly is indeed one of the major social problems facing our country in the years ahead, and it is certain to affect all of us.

The Growing Elderly Population

There are nearly twenty-five million people age sixty-five or older in America today, comprising over 11% of the population.

By the year 2030, however, their numbers are expected to double to fifty-five million people, or more than 18% of the population. By then, an astounding one out of every five persons will be a senior citizen.

Part of the reason for this is the movement of aging baby boomers into the ranks of the senior citizen. Another is the rise in life expectancy, which is currently 74.7 years, an increase of five years over the previous generation. Improved medical care and adjustments in lifestyle (such as regular exercise and changes in diet) have helped the elderly live longer, more productive lives. But the problem arises of how to properly care for this ever-growing segment of society.

THE PROBLEMS OF THE ELDERLY

Many of us assume that since the elderly have had a lifetime of earning, they have been able to save a comfortable nest egg for their retirement. But as a group, senior citizens may be the poorest around. Almost half of all those seventy-five or older have to subsist on incomes or Social Security checks that are well below the poverty line. For men over sixty-five, that adds up to a median income of $10,450 a year, and for women it's even lower— $6,020. Ironically, seniors' incomes are reduced at the time of life when their need for costly extra services (medical care, hospitalization, physical assistance) is the greatest.

Medical Care

The real strain, of course, comes in paying for medical treatment for the common ailments associated with advanced age, such as arthritis, hypertension, and hearing and visual impairments. Many of these problems can be controlled with prescribed medication, but with meager Social Security checks, some seniors are unable to afford even the visits to the doctors' offices, let alone the cost of medication.

The problem is compounded with the onset of more major physical disabilities—diabetes, heart disease, cancer, Alzheimer's —for which surgery and extended hospitalization are usually required. Medicare and Medicaid pick up a large part of the bill, but more and more, the elderly are being asked to assume a greater share of the costs. One study claims that despite the assistance of

Medicare and Medicaid, the elderly spend as much now on medical care as they did before these programs were established: about $1,000 a year.

Housing

Among those who are seventy-five or older, nearly 70% live in their own homes. However, most of the elderly are physically and financially unable to keep them up. A study during the 1970s showed that about a quarter of all the homes owned by seniors had serious problems, such as leaking roofs, unvented room heaters, and inadequate plumbing and electrical wiring. In rural areas, the percentage was even higher, almost 35%. By living in unhealthy and unsafe houses, the elderly increase their chances of having an accident or getting sick, yet moving out of their homes is so emotionally trying that it often leads to depression. Many of the elderly who cannot afford to own their own homes live in apartments or government-subsidized housing, which are often located in lower-income urban areas. In these high-crime locations, the elderly are especially vulnerable to robbery, rape and home intrusion. As a result, many seniors rarely leave their homes.

Nursing Homes

We often think of the elderly as living in nursing homes, but in fact only about 5% of those over sixty-five do so; for those over eighty-five, the percentage increases to one in five. But as the size of the senior population rapidly increases, so too will the number of elderly living in such institutions. About a million and a half senior citizens currently live in nursing homes, but by the year 2040, that number is expected to expand to twenty million. Extended nursing home care is not covered by most health care plans, including HMOs, and Medicare pays only a small part of the bill (up to twenty-seven days annually). Lacking the funds to live in nursing homes, the elderly are forced to liquidate their assets in order to qualify for Medicaid assistance.

Affordability is not the only hurdle the elderly face in seeking nursing home care. Half of the nation's nursing homes have waiting lists, with a median waiting time of almost six months for a semi-private room. In New York State, some senior citizens have lived in hospitals for as long as a year and a half waiting for a space to open up in a nursing home. The problem will surely worsen as the senior population grows.

Alcoholism

The elderly alcoholic may be one of society's best kept secrets. Having long ignored the problems of senior citizens in favor of those of younger age groups, we are just now beginning to focus on the plight of the elderly. And we are finding that many, over one million by some estimates, are turning to alcohol to alleviate depression and loneliness. The drinking is only worsening their situation, contributing to ailments that often led them to drink in the first place, such as memory loss, paralysis, peripheral nerve problems, liver and kidney ailments, and broken bones.

Suicide

When we consider suicides, most of us think of teenagers. But in fact, suicide rates among the elderly are higher than for any other age group. Some studies indicate that 25% of all suicides in the U.S. are committed by senior citizens; other experts estimate that it may be as high as 30% to 40%. They cite feelings often expressed by the elderly, such as uselessness, loneliness, and boredom, as well as economic worries and the loss of loved ones, as reasons.

Abuse and Neglect

While the abuse and neglect of children has received a great deal of press over the last few years, the same problem among the elderly population has rarely been publicized. An estimated 10% of those over sixty-five are abused in some way every year.

Abuse among the elderly is manifested by physical, sexual, psychological or medical abuse, as well as by financial exploitation and/or neglect. Such treatment often comes at the hands of relatives, family friends, or professional caregivers, who either inflict pain or withhold needed care. The latter, known as passive neglect, in which a person knowingly fails to keep an elderly person clean or well-fed, is the most common form of mistreatment. Aggressive abuse—physical, sexual, or psychological—is not as prevalent, but it still affects as many as one in twenty-five seniors.

GETTING INVOLVED AS A VOLUNTEER

Our nation is slowly gearing up to face the problems associated with a growing elderly population, but you can make a personal difference in the lives of seniors now. Below are listed a number of human services for the elderly which need the support and assistance of volunteers.

A Volunteer and His Dog

Ron had occasionally thought about visiting nursing homes as a volunteer, but he "had never done anything serious about it." Like everybody else, he had "a million and one things to do," and it seemed as if he "never had enough time to get things done." But when he was moved to the evening shift at work, he suddenly found himself with a lot of free time during the day.

An animal lover, Ron found out about the Pet Therapy program in the newsletter of the Animal Protective Association, which he had donated to regularly over the years. He thought that his dog Annie, a part sheltie mix, might be good for the program, since she herself was handicapped, having only three legs. "I thought that the people would like to see how well a dog could adapt to a handicap and that it might help them. And since Annie is very good with people and very friendly, I volunteered."

Four times a month Ron takes Annie to nursing homes, talking to the patients while letting them pet or hold Annie. "Annie gets along well with the people, and she's small enough that many times you can put her in a person's lap or up on their bed." The people in the homes can become very attached to Annie. Ron tells the story of one woman who didn't want the dog to leave. "She asked if she could hold her. I said sure and put Annie in her lap. I noticed that after a few minutes that Annie was still there, and she had the funniest look on her face. The lady was saying, 'Oh, Annie just loves to be with me, she really just doesn't want to leave me.' When I looked down, I saw that the lady had her finger hooked underneath Annie's collar so she couldn't get down." For Ron, the story is a bittersweet example of how much the program means to the patients. "They are so starved for affection," he says. "I think that bringing little Annie into their life and just sitting and talking to them makes life a little cheerier."

Outreach Programs

Outreach provides needed services and support to shut-in elderly persons. One popular program, Meals on Wheels, is a nationwide program which prepares meals free of charge for anyone over sixty years old. Prepared five to seven days a week by both paid and volunteer workers, the meals are either served at public locations (usually in senior centers) or delivered directly to the homebound. In 1984, 230,000 volunteers were involved in the Meals on Wheels program. Other voluntary organizations, such as Sisters' Care in St. Paul and the Philadelphia Geriatric Center, provide in-home services to senior citizens. Volunteers visit the elderly at their homes, do their shopping for them, and deliver medicine and other necessities. Some organizations, such as the American Red Cross, have telephone reassurance programs for the elderly which are staffed by volunteers. Other programs, such as Neighbors Helping Neighbors in Chicago, match a volunteer with an elderly person for friendship and support.

Senior Centers

Senior centers, adult day-care centers, and nursing homes allow volunteers to use their skills and hobbies to enrich the lives of others. Depending on the services offered by the organization chosen, volunteers may find themselves leading activities such as arts and crafts, forming discussion groups on current events, announcing Bingo games, planning field trips, or simply visiting with members. Volunteers with talents in music, hair styling, and arts and crafts are in great demand.

Some senior centers that use volunteers offer comprehensive support services for the elderly. Centers run by Catholic Charities offer recreational, educational, preventive health and personal care services. The Salvation Army through its senior citizen's centers uses volunteers to organize outings for seniors and to assist in visitation programs and homemaker projects.

Transportation

Many community agencies and national organizations, such as the American Red Cross and the Salvation Army, depend on the help of volunteer drivers to transport senior citizens to medical appointments, shopping centers, and community services. Volunteers usually drive small vans provided by the agency and follow a planned, organized route.

Legal Assistance

Public benefit programs, age discrimination, supplemental security income, consumer or housing problems, wills and pro-

---

"Do You Have One Hour A Week To Help A Homebound Elderly Person?"

That's what the flyers posted around strategic sections of the city ask passersby. Aware that people who want to volunteer have only a limited amount of time to do so, Anita Katz, head of the Neighbors Helping Neighbors program which matches volunteers with elderly shut-ins, decided to limit the commitment to one hour a week.

When first setting up the Neighbors program, Anita talked with corporate leaders, looking to gain some insight into how she might develop a program that would make it easier for people who have full-time careers to volunteer. The discussions focused on time. "They told us that they would love their employees to be volunteers and be community-minded, but that most institutions demanded a lot of time. Hospitals and nursing homes, particularly, seemed to be asking for a whole day. And here is a population of people who are upwardly mobile, who have professional careers and personal lives, and yet they want to do something. So, we thought instead of saying can you give a day or your whole life or whatever, why don't we just say one hour?" The good number of people who have signed up is an indication that limiting the volunteer's commitment to that hour has been a major reason behind the program's success.

Further experience has shown that an hour, besides being convenient for volunteers, is also best for the elderly. "A frail elderly person may not need much more than an hour or so of visitation," Anita says. "We want the volunteer to bring some kind of happiness and lightness into that individual's life for a certain amount of time. [The elderly] don't need a marathon association most of the time. And people get tired, especially the elderly." The program is now five years old, and the way it is set up, Anita believes, allows people to "have it all: you can do something that is very worthwhile and still have the kind of activities in your life that you want to have." All for one hour a week.

bate: these are all common problems for the elderly, especially those without money and supportive families. Lawyers or legal aids can volunteer their time to help seniors deal with these issues and learn about their rights. Bar associations have recently begun responding to these needs. Thirty-three state bar associations and other pro-bono organizations have banded together to offer legal assistance to senior citizens in the form of handbooks, education, and legal counsel.

SENIOR VOLUNTEERS HELPING OTHERS IN NEED

Senior citizens often find fulfillment by participating in a variety of volunteer programs themselves.

Peer Counseling

Senior citizens may want to consider peer counseling. Many communities have set up counseling centers where trained volunteers in or approaching retirement age can listen and counsel those who are having trouble coping with personal problems. The grief of losing a spouse or family member, families moving away, or the dwindling of a circle of friends is difficult to bear alone. Yet many who have lived their lives without seeking psychological help are reluctant to ask for it later in life. Peer counseling offers these seniors an alternative. Volunteers and participants in programs such as Baltimore's Peers in Passage have found that the process helps people on both sides to resolve problems and unearth personal strengths.

On a larger scale, the American Association of Retired Persons (AARP), offers opportunities such as Tax-Aide and Medicare assistance volunteers. With more than twenty-eight million members, AARP's Volunteer Talent Bank has thousands of volunteer positions for seniors who want to work with their peers.

Federal Volunteer Programs

In 1984 over 383,000 senior citizens participated in one of the following federal programs funded by the Older American Volunteer Programs (or ACTION): *Foster Grandparents Program*, in which low-income seniors work with disadvantaged, handicapped, or abused children for a small stipend; *Senior Companion Program,* in which volunteers help the homebound or nursing home residents by visiting and running small errands; *Retired Senior Volunteer Program,* in which seniors work in public organizations such as schools, courts, libraries and museums assuming various duties; and *Service Corps of Retired Executives,* in which owners of small businesses or community groups are matched with elderly volunteers who share the wisdom they gained through their own experience in business. Through *VISTA* and the *Peace Corps* seniors can also volunteer for two months to two years to work in poor American communities or in developing countries on projects instituted by these larger organizations.

AARP: "To serve, not to be served"

With a roster of twenty-eight million members, the American Association of Retired Persons, AARP, is the largest non-profit, non-partisan membership organization in the world. Founded in 1958 by Dr. Ethel Percy Andrus, AARP seeks to improve the quality of life and promote independence and dignity for senior citizens.

Through 3,700 local chapters nationwide, AARP's staff and 400,000 volunteers deliver a variety of services to older Americans. AARP's health advocate volunteers give health care seminars and assist seniors in filing Medicaid and Medicare claims. Some AARP volunteers give seniors instruction on crime prevention, while others teach driver education, provide housing assistance, or offer free income-tax counseling services to older Americans.

AARP volunteers are also active in lobbying for seniors. Focusing on issues such as Social Security, pension legislation, health care reform, civil rights, and social service programs, AARP volunteers advocate on both a national and local level.

For older Americans, AARP not only provides numerous services, but many opportunities to serve as well. AARP's Volunteer Talent Bank offers older volunteers opportunities with both AARP programs and with other organizations as well. Through its large volunteer corp, AARP lives up to its motto, "To serve, not to be served."

Advocacy

For seniors who are concerned with issues such as social security, nursing home reform, and age discrimination, organizations such as AARP, the Gray Panthers, and the Older Woman's League could use your help. Volunteers are needed to write letters, raise funds, organize local groups and perform other types of advocacy work.

VOLUNTEERING TO HELP THE ELDERLY

Whether you are a senior citizen or a teenager, volunteering to assist the elderly is one of the most rewarding areas of volunteer work. If you are interested in sharing your love and care with senior citizens, consult the directory at the end of this book for the name and address of a clearinghouse in your area.

THE FOSTER GRANDPARENT PROGRAM

Of the three Older American Volunteer programs operated by ACTION (the federally-sponsored National Volunteer Agency), the Foster Grandparent Program is probably the best known. Since its founding in 1965, the program has established more than 250 projects in all fifty states, with over 16,000 volunteers.

The Foster Grandparent Program pairs volunteers age sixty or over with children who are either physically handicapped, mentally retarded, or abused and neglected. Volunteers usually work within institutions or hospital settings, giving children the individual attention hospital staffs and parents are unable to provide. The Grandparents are assigned to two children, which they visit on a regular basis for two-hour periods. The nature of the work depends greatly on the problems of the children, but the role of the volunteer is "to be a grandparent in every possible sense—a caring, stable presence in a child's life."

The program is open only to the low-income elderly, which receive a small stipend for their services, as well as transportation costs, meals while on service, accident insurance, and annual physical examinations. Volunteers are required to attend twenty to forty hours of in-service training and monthly training programs.

CHAPTER THIRTEEN

Battered Women

WITH HER LIFE centered around the community and the parish church, Karen was well aware of the problems confronting people in their everyday lives. Or so she thought, until she signed up to volunteer at a local shelter for battered women. Working at the shelter as a crisis counselor for the last two years, Karen has come to see firsthand "the extent of real, domestic violence that people live with in this society." And it has been an unpleasant surprise. She, along with other volunteers, handles the flood of calls from women who have been abused by their husbands and boyfriends, listening to their horrific stories and steering them to help. The shelter's thirty beds are almost always filled, and an average of five women are turned away from the shelter every day for lack of room. The misery she sees and hears at the shelter on a daily basis has made Karen realize just how large and widespread the problem of abuse truly is.

For those of us who have never worked at a shelter, statistics can give us a less personal, but no less incredible, idea of the extent of wife abuse. Three to four million women are battered each year, nearly a third of whom are so badly beaten that they must seek medical care. Of course, these are just estimates; most women are too scared or too apprehensive of police protection to lodge complaints against their batterers. Thus, the actual number of battered women may be much, much higher. It's not surprising that battery is the single greatest cause of injury to women in the United States, even more than injuries due to automobile accidents.

Physically weaker and victims of a society that has until recently denied them their rights, women are almost always the targets in battering cases. Between 85% and 95% of all assault victims are female, as are two-thirds of all domestic murder

149

victims. More than 50% of the female victims are battered or killed by people they know, usually boyfriends or spouses. In 1985 alone, over 15,000 women were killed by their husbands, former spouses, or boyfriends. Indeed, marriage seems to offer many women little refuge from such violence. Some surveys indicate that one in every four married couples experience at least one serious incident of domestic violence.

WHAT IS ABUSE?

Although the terms "violence," "abuse," "battery," and "assault" are often used interchangeably, their meanings are quite different. "Violence" refers to physical force, while "abuse" can include both non-violent and violent interaction. The word "assault" alone is used when a victim fears bodily or emotional harm; "battery" refers to the actual blow or physical abuse. Hence, the term "assault and battery," is used when a person is the victim of both physical and verbal abuse.

BACKGROUND

A study of family violence was begun in the 1960s as part of a larger research project on physical assault across the nation. At that time there were almost no reported cases of woman abuse, and those that existed were attributed to personality disorders in both the men and women involved. Violence in families was thought to be infrequent and was considered the result of restricted individual psychopathology that had few ramifications within society. It wasn't until the early 1970s when sociologists started to study family violence on a broader scale that they saw just how widespread and pervasive the problem really was. Today with increased media exposure of the issue through such cases as the Joel Steinberg and Hedda Nussbaum trial, more and more people are becoming aware of just how serious the problem of female battery is, and they are becoming more actively involved in alleviating it.

THE BATTERED WOMAN

For those on the outside, it is hard to fathom why an abused woman would not simply escape from her situation. It was once thought that the battered woman remained because she felt responsible for the abuse—that she was somehow a bad wife or mother, or because she actually liked the abuse. But as more research was done on the issue of domestic violence, it became more apparent that battered women tend to be physically, financially, and emotionally dependent on their abusers. A woman may put up with abuse because she cannot overcome the belief that the man is the only breadwinner in the family and that if she were to leave, she would be unable to support herself.

Fear also plays a major role. A woman may stay in an abusive home because of fear of the unknown outside world or fear that the batterer will come after her. Although she may realize that staying puts her life and the lives of her children in danger, she is more afraid of the loneliness, financial devastation, failure, and possible loss of friends that could result from leaving. That fear is often so strong that a woman will stay even when her children become involved in the abuse.

WHAT IS BEING DONE

In an attempt to stem the rash of domestic violence, many states and cities have passed mandatory arrest laws, which force police to arrest men accused of battering their wives or other women. Under these laws, which exist in eleven states and a number of cities, police have to arrest the batterer, even if the woman, neighbor, or relative lodging the complaint only wants the batterer to be given a warning or taken from the home. The police are under orders to jail the offender for at least one night.

Most of the assistance to battered women, however, comes in the form of shelters and crisis hotlines. The National Coalition Against Domestic Violence was one of the first major organizations to help abused women across the country. They established a network of shelters and walk-in agencies to give physical and legal assistance to battered women. The coalition also operates a twenty-four-hour crisis hotline, manned by volunteers.

There are more than 1,000 shelters nationwide, some of which receive limited funding from the Department of Human Services, state branches of The National Coalition Against Domestic Violence, and private sources and donations. Shelters often provide up to thirty days of shelter for a woman and her children (sometimes for a nominal fee), in addition to counseling, extended social service, and legal assistance. They will often help get a woman to a hospital, find an apartment, and apply for welfare. Additional services include public education efforts and the training of law enforcement officials and legal personnel on the problem of domestic violence.

Due to the lack of funding from the federal and state governments, however, most shelters are started and supported by local grassroots movements or community outreach programs. The Neopolitan Lighthouse in Chicago, for example, originally started out as a Safe Homes program, which used the homes of volunteers to temporarily house battered women and their children. Once funding became available, the Lighthouse project was established and a regular shelter was built. A paid professional staff member was hired, but the majority of the work is still carried out by volunteers. In fact, most shelters for women, like the Neopolitan Lighthouse, would not be able to survive were it not for the help of volunteers.

THE WORK OF THE VOLUNTEER

A volunteer's efforts are usually concentrated in four areas: manning a hotline, working around a shelter, assisting with a children's program, or providing legal assistance.

Hotlines

When a battered woman calls a crisis hotline, a volunteer determines the physical and emotional state of the caller in order to steer her to the type of help she may need. The volunteer then identifies the various options open to her, such as calling the police, leaving the house, staying with friends, or coming to a shelter, and then provides her with information on the shelter's services.

At the Shelter

The opportunities for volunteers who are working at a shelter include running the front desk (where they can help residents take advantage of the shelter's services and facilities); driving women to local social service agencies, courts, and hospitals; and helping maintain the shelter. Volunteers can also work at "information booths" or serve as counselors, giving battered women information about their legal rights, job opportunities, and the availability of other social services. "A volunteer can do just about anything around the shelter from helping residents with laundry tokens to giving information on how to get to Domestic Violence Court," says Julie Eskenazi, former Volunteer and Education Coordinator for the Greenhouse Shelter. After volunteers have become familiar with the shelter and have worked there for a few months, they can then begin to assist as fundraisers, recruiters of new volunteers, organizers of support groups, and public speakers. They can also become involved as child advocates, planning and running children activities. "The sky is the limit" on the number of ways a volunteer can get involved," says Julie.

Legal Assistance

Since most crisis hotline callers ask questions regarding their legal rights, all volunteers are given the basic information concerning the rights of battered women. However, there are also opportunities for lawyers and others without legal training to serve as legal advocates.

BECOMING A VOLUNTEER

The easiest way of becoming a volunteer at a women's shelter is to contact your city's volunteer clearinghouse listed in *The Good Heart Book's* directory. The clearinghouse will be able to steer you to a local women's shelter. Most shelters will require you to fill out an application and attend an informal interview. You will most likely be asked to attend a training seminar and, upon completing it, to make a long-term commitment to working at the shelter. Women's shelters have little funding, limited resources, and small staffs, and they consequently cannot afford to invest both time and money in training volunteers who will only be involved for a few weeks.

The Training Program

Generally, volunteers attend a comprehensive training program, which consists of lectures, discussions, and films explaining the issue of abuse and the philosophy of the shelter. The training programs are usually mandatory and are extended over a number of sessions.

New volunteers at the Greenhouse Shelter must undergo forty hours of training. The forty hours is comprised of four, seven hour sessions of lectures and small group discussions, which are held on Saturdays. The balance of the training period is spent observing experienced volunteers at work in the shelter during the week. For the program to be at all effective, the directors of the

On the Front Lines: The Crisis Hotline Counselor

The phones usually ring off the hook at the Evanston Shelter for Battered Women. As a crisis line worker there, Karen's job is to handle all incoming calls, which range from callers wanting to make donations or get information to troubled women needing help and shelter from abusive husbands and boyfriends. Before addressing the immediate problems, Karen must gather a form's worth of information, such as the caller's location, her condition as well as that of any children, and the involvement of the police. Karen then informs the caller of her rights.

But much of her work centers around just talking to the callers about their problems and getting them the services they need. The calls are emotionally demanding and the paper work tedious, and Karen often feels drained after her weekly three-hour shift. But she feels good about her work and the commitment to "doing something to make a difference." Three years of experience at the shelter has helped her to communicate with callers more effectively, and she has broadened her knowledge of the numerous resources to which she can refer them. But despite all her training and background, Karen has found that the thing she has learned the most "is that [she is] always learning."

shelter feel that a six-month commitment must be made and that volunteers should put in at least four hours a week.

Getting Involved

The picture of the cut and swollen face of Hedda Nussbaum during the Joel Steinberg trial again brought the reality of woman abuse to the front pages of the newspapers and weekly magazines. But for every woman who is helped at a shelter, there are hundreds more who are turned away due to lack of facilities and volunteer support. Four hundred abused women and children are turned away from shelters every week in Chicago alone. Volunteers are crucial to the survival of hotlines and shelters across the country, and the need for them has never been greater.

CHAPTER FOURTEEN

People With AIDS (PWAs)

T HE FACES in Nicholas Nixon's recent photographic exhibition of AIDS victims, or PWAs (People With AIDS) as activists prefer to call them, are haunting. Most are skeletal, with skin pulled tight across the forehead and cheek bones, hanging loose in the jowls, seeming to pull their frowns down even further. But it is the eyes that tell you the most. They stare back at you, blank and shrunken in their sockets, seeing no hope and no future. And, indeed, as of yet there is none. These men are dying, and their hopelessness is seen in their faces.

But what truly makes these pictures so haunting is that the faces look so familiar. They are not exotic or foreign or somehow different from us. These are the faces that are so much a part of our everyday lives—of friends, family members, of people we pass daily in the street. We may not know these victims personally, but in Nixon's pictures we recognize their humanity, the tie that binds us to them. And it's in that recognition that we feel sorrow for these people and are moved by their suffering, sometimes even enough to reach out and help them.

A GROWING EPIDEMIC

AIDS is spreading so quickly that by 1992 each one of us will personally know someone who has died from AIDS. A staggering number have died already. As of February 1990, 121,645 AIDS cases have been diagnosed, a number that is expected to triple by 1992, according to the Centers for Disease Control. Of the diagnosed cases, more than 30,000 PWAs have died so far, making AIDS one of the leading causes of death among men between 25 and 44 years of age. And these numbers do not even include the 1.5 million people who are latent carriers of the AIDS virus but don't yet display any of the symptoms. These statistics become even more powerful when read in the light of the grim fact that no one has been cured and there is no cure in sight.

WHAT IS AIDS?

AIDS, the acronym for Acquired Immune Deficiency Syndrome, is a disease caused by the Human Immunodeficiency Virus (HIV), which attacks the body's immune system by destroying infection-fighting white blood cells. By killing these cells, the HIV, although not deadly in itself, denies the body the capability to defend itself from even the slightest infection. Consequently, PWAs normally die from complications relating to infection, including pneumonia, meningitis, and rare forms of cancer.

The disease itself is spread through an exchange of the body's fluids, such as saliva, blood, semen, and vaginal secretions. This exchange frequently occurs during sexual contact and the sharing of contaminated needles. Of all reported cases, over 90% became infected with the AIDS virus from one of these situations. Although people from every race and walk of life have contracted the disease, those with a high risk of becoming infected include male homosexuals and bisexuals and intravenous drug users. Among other groups affected to a lesser extent are people who have received infected blood samples during transfusions and babies born to mothers infected with AIDS. The incidence of AIDS among the heterosexual population is increasing.

WHAT IS BEING DONE
The Federal Government

The Centers for Disease Control, the branch of the Public Health Service that is responsible for the prevention and control of diseases through research, testing, and education, spends approximately $2 million a year to combat AIDS. An increase in funding is expected, although many legislators are reluctant to allocate too large a sum, convinced that simply spending more money will not solve the problem. Under the aegis of C. Everett Koop, former Surgeon General, the Center launched a massive public information campaign, distributing free pamphlets on AIDS, including "Facts About AIDS," "How You Won't Get

AIDS," the "Surgeon General's Report on AIDS," and "Understanding AIDS," a brochure sent to every resident of the United States. The National AIDS Information Clearinghouse

Women With AIDS

When we think of groups of people that have AIDS, those that come most readily to mind are homosexuals, intravenous drug abusers, maybe hemophiliacs. Not many of us think of women. And until recently, there has not been much of a reason to do so. But as the AIDS epidemic has spread, there is mounting evidence that a growing number of women are becoming infected with the deadly HIV virus.

According to figures recently released by the Centers for Disease Control, over 8,100 women have been diagnosed as having AIDS, and thousands more are suspected of carrying HIV, the AIDS virus. As a group, women with AIDS is the fastest growing of all AIDS categories. The majority, over 52%, have contracted the virus through intravenous drug use, but a growing number are becoming infected through sexual contact: nearly 18% from sex with an IV drug user, 3.3% from sex with bisexual males, and 3.9% from other forms of heterosexual contact. Infection through sexual contact has increased so dramatically that up to a third of all women with the virus contract it in this way.

What is so disturbing about these statistics is that so little is known about women and AIDS—how they are infected, why their symptoms are different from those of men with AIDS, why they die so much quicker than their male counterparts. Indeed, so little is known about women with AIDS that many doctors are unable to diagnose the virus when they see it. The problem has many ramifications. First, there are a lot of dying women out there who have no idea what's wrong with them. In one study, two-thirds of the women diagnosed with AIDS never suspected that they could get it. Then there are the nearly 1,500 babies who became infected with the virus from their mothers. There is also the on-going attempt to prevent the spread of AIDS: doctors cannot effectively limit spreading until they understand how it affects all people—both men and women.

From "Women and AIDS: The Hidden Toll," by Mary Schmich and John Van, *Chicago Tribune.* Copyrighted, Chicago Tribune Company. All rights reserved. Used with permission.

provides the public with free copies of these government documents.

State and Local Governments

Few state or city governments have comprehensive AIDS policies at this time. In large urban areas like Los Angeles, Philadelphia, and Chicago, programs have been established to deal only with aspects of the AIDS problem, such as homeless PWAs, AIDS education in the public schools, and medical care for PWAs.

New York City, however, which is home to an estimated 25% of the nation's full-scale AIDS patients, has recently announced a comprehensive program to deal with the AIDS crisis. The city has allocated $180 million for hospital care, research, education, and testing programs. The initiative also provides rent subsidies and a shelter for homeless PWAs.

Strains on the System

Despite the efforts of a network of public and private agencies across the country, the AIDS epidemic is growing at a pace faster than the human care system can cope with it. Hospitals are quickly becoming overwhelmed by the needs of PWAs, and many are chronically short of hospital beds and medical facilities to treat them. In New York City, where the hospital occupancy rate is already 95%, experts predict that by 1992, 40% of the hospital beds will be filled by AIDS patients.

The cost of treating PWAs, as much as $800 a patient per day, is also a major problem for the health care system. Already faced with skyrocketing health care costs, many hospitals are unable to accept PWAs who don't have health insurance. This has forced the health industry to come up with viable alternative forms of care. More and more are turning to volunteers to continue providing care to a segment of the population greatly in need of it.

VOLUNTEERING TO ASSIST PWAs

To assist the overburdened governmental agencies and health care system in handling the AIDS crisis, a number of private, non-profit agencies have sprung up across the country. These groups provide such needed services as shelter and meals, legal aid, counseling groups, and toll-free AIDS hotlines. Among the national groups providing extended assistance to PWAs are the Red Cross, the Human Rights Campaign Fund, and the American Foundation for AIDS Research.

In most major urban areas, local groups also provide comprehensive services. The San Francisco AIDS Foundation and New York City's AIDS Resource Center offer programs for PWAs, their families, and the public. To help prevent the spread of AIDS, these organizations print literature, give educational talks in schools, and run workshops and seminars for health and counseling professionals.

Working with PWAs

According to all medical studies, you cannot become infected with AIDS except through sexual contact or the sharing of contaminated needles. AIDS is not spread through casual contact, including non-sexual kissing or the sharing of cups, eating utensils, toothbrushes, or food. Nevertheless, volunteers should exercise caution when caring for PWAs. They should take care to avoid being stuck with needles used by AIDS patients or to allow blood to enter an open wound or cut.

Hotlines and Public Information Campaigns

Volunteers are used in a number of different capacities, which depend on the nature of the organization. Those without a medical background most frequently work on AIDS hotlines or in public information campaigns. The National Hotline on AIDS (1-800-342-AIDS), in English, Spanish, and for the hearing impaired, is the only official national AIDS organization. Volunteers manning hotline telephones provide callers with information about AIDS symptoms, means of transmission and prevention, as well as referral to clinics and hospice units caring for PWAs. Hotline volunteers also give information on other sexually transmitted diseases and drug abuse, and they serve as crisis counselors for callers contemplating suicide.

Community outreach programs use volunteers in public information campaigns to distribute literature and answer questions in informal settings. In one program, for example, volunteers worked at an AIDS information table in a local bowling alley for a week handing out free pamphlets and answering questions. The same organization has also designed a three-hour discussion program on AIDS prevention, which is available free of charge to local civic groups. Volunteers are used in the office to help with the scheduling of events, phone and paper work, and mailings. Volunteers can work in the evenings from 7:00 to 10:00 or during the day, when additional help is needed the most.

Volunteer Caretakers

Volunteers are also used in programs catering to the needs of hospitalized or homebound PWAs. Home visitors normally check on PWAs once or twice a week to talk and help them with tasks they can no longer perform. Assisting homebound PWAs can include delivering groceries or medicine, cleaning house, and changing sheets.

Hospice volunteers assist nurses in caring for hospitalized PWAs. They feed, clean, and console patients. They also give emotional support to the family and friends of the PWA. One volunteer group, the Hospice Volunteers of Dupage County, gives workshops to family members and friends of PWAs on death and the grieving process.

NATIONAL AIDS NETWORK (NAN)

The National AIDS Network (NAN) grew out of the need for a central institution which would serve as a networking and resource agency for the hundreds of community-based organizations combatting the AIDS crisis. Now seven years old, the Network supports the efforts of 650 local service providers, serving as a center where they can interact and share information, technical expertise, and their experiences. NAN also provides a wealth of communications and resource materials, including two bi-monthly newsletters, *Network News* and *Multi-Cultural NOTES,* as well as the *NAN Directory of AIDS Education and Service Organizations,* a comprehensive listing of organizations servicing the needs of PWAs. Additional support comes in the form of training programs and media campaigns.

For more information, contact: National AIDS Network, 2033 M Street, N.W., Suite 800, Washington, DC 20036 (202) 293-2437.

Legal Volunteers

Lawyers can volunteer to provide legal assistance for AIDS victims, either through their own firms or through local AIDS legal organizations, such as Chicago's AIDS Legal Council. Volunteer lawyers are used to help AIDS victims with the emotionally difficult and normally costly legal services they need, such as getting medical benefits, fighting job and housing discrimination, making out a will, and settling financial affairs.

TRAINING FOR AIDS VOLUNTEERS

The training for assisting PWAs varies according to the services an organization provides. One night of training is all that is required for volunteers to familiarize themselves with the issue of AIDS and the mission of Stop AIDS Chicago. Harbor Homes Support Service's training program, on the other hand, which is typical of many that help homebound patients, is much more extensive. Volunteers in groups of about ten attend twenty hours of training, which is usually held over the course of one weekend. On the first evening, prospective volunteers are given background information on AIDS, including a history of the illness, the sociology and epidemiology of the HIV, modes of transmission, stages of the illness and other basic AIDS information. When the volunteers return the next day, they learn aspects of caring for homebound AIDS patients, such as how to bathe them. They are also shown how to take safety precautions when handling PWAs.

THE AIDS VOLUNTEER

The common denominator among volunteers working to assist PWAs is the belief that those stricken with AIDS should not die alone and that they deserve help regardless of their situation. And as the AIDS crisis escalates, the need for concerned, compassionate volunteers will only become greater.

CHAPTER FIFTEEN

People With Disabilities

FOR MOST OF US, the word "handicapped" or "disabled" brings to mind people bound to wheelchairs, who have special ramps in buildings and allotted parking spaces nearest the entrances of stores and shopping centers. But as a term, handicapped covers a larger group than just invalids: it includes the thirty-six million Americans with such disabilities as blindness, deafness, neurological dysfunctions, and orthopedic defects. Among the adults in this group, almost eight million are immobile or severely limited in walking, nearly seven million are blind or have severely limited vision, nearly six million have some degree of mental retardation, and half a million are deaf or greatly restricted in their hearing. Indeed, the Americans living with physical and mental impairments have been called our largest and last minority, reflecting both their size as a group as well as their struggle to attain basic civil rights as other minorities before them have done.

WHAT IT MEANS TO HAVE DISABILITIES

Having a disability not only means having to suffer from a physical or mental impairment; it also means having to lead a life that is limited in breadth. Unable to find work, gain access to buildings without special facilities, or attend recreational events without being stared at or taunted, people with disabilities indeed suffer under more than just the physical aspects of their handicaps.

Unfortunately, for many individuals with disabilities, society's prejudice often hinders them more than the disability itself. This prejudice is most visible in the workplace. A person who is blind, deaf, or crippled still has all of his or her other faculties and can successfully handle many jobs if given the opportunity. However, the Center for the Study of Social Policy reports that an estimated 12.3 million employable adults who have disabilities are unable to gain any employment. Of the five million that do hold jobs, according to one report, the majority are working beneath their capabilities.

This group also faces discrimination in other areas. Many communities have passed zoning laws prohibiting the development of group homes for people with disabilities, housing which would allow them to live independently. Some people refuse to socialize with them. Even worse, many of the individuals who have disabilities begin to adopt society's prejudice as their own, believing that they are "different" and unable to do normal things. These are the real handicaps that people with disabilities face on a daily basis, those things that limit their opportunity to take part in the community on an equal level with others.

The goal of this group and its advocates is to close the gap between the physical, psychological, educational, and social barriers that keep the handicapped situation alive. To accomplish this, they need assistance. They need increased governmental and educational programs that encourage rehabilitation and self-sufficiency; they need increased opportunities for employment; and most importantly, they need concerned people to help change society's image of people who have disabilities if they are to become fully integrated into society.

CAUSES OF DISABILITY

The causes of disabilities are numerous. Neurological dysfunctions, diseases that affect the brain, nervous system, or muscles, are the largest single cause. Some of these dysfunctions occur as birth defects, affecting three out of every 100 babies born in America. Of these, Cerebral Palsy, which is usually caused by prenatal damage to the brain, is the most common. By attacking the nerves that control the body's muscles, the disease causes spastic paralysis, tremors, and poor coordination.

Mental retardation, which affects over 100,000 newborn babies annually, can also occur after birth. Well over 250 causes of mental retardation have been discovered. Poor prenatal care, maternal malnutrition, and a pregnant mother's use of drugs or alcohol can result in a baby being born retarded. Causes of mental retardation after birth include lead poisoning, childhood diseases such as chicken pox and measles, and even lack of mental stimulation and parental affection.

Other major neurological dysfunctions include Down's Syndrome, a birth defect, and Muscular Dystrophy, which affects both children and teenagers. Down's Syndrome is a disease that affects the brain, causing physical malformations and mental retardation. Muscular Dystrophy attacks the body's muscles, resulting in a gradual weakening and wasting away of the muscle tissue.

Multiple Sclerosis affects the body's nervous system, which leads to tremors, speech deficiencies, vision impairment and sometimes paralysis. Other neurological dysfunctions include polio, epilepsy, and mental retardation.

Vision and hearing impairments are another cause of disablement, affecting over two million Americans. Diseases such as glaucoma and mastoiditis, infections, and side effects from some neurological disorders can also result in other impairments.

SPECIAL OLYMPICS

Held every four years, the Special Olympics gives developmentally disabled adults and children an opportunity to utilize their skills and talents in competitive sporting events. Founded on the belief that people with disabilities can learn and benefit from participation in individual and team sports, the event encourages people with disabilities to believe that they can still participate in life.

The last Special Olympics was held in 1987 on the campuses of Notre Dame University and St. Mary's College. The 5,000 participants came from all fifty states and seventy foreign countries. Over 23,000 volunteers participated in putting on the event, from raising $6 million to officiating and managing all aspects of running a major sporting event. They timed the races, ran refreshment stands, accompanied the athletes, and most importantly, enthusiastically cheered on the disabled athletes.

Local Special Olympics and similar events are held across the country. If you are interested in participating as a volunteer, contact your local clearinghouse for information on how to sign up.

Another major cause of disabilities are orthopedic dysfunctions and injuries. These are often the result of diseases that affect the body's bones and joints, manifesting themselves in severe arthritis, rheumatism, and chronic bursitis. They can also be the result of accidents or war injuries. The symptoms of these orthopedic dysfunctions and injuries include constant pain, limitations in mobility, and in severe cases, paralysis.

TREATMENT OF DISABILITIES

In recent years the medical profession has made enormous progress in treating and caring for people with disabilities. Vaccines have made some diseases, such as polio, much less common, and medications have been created that reduce the disabling impact of epilepsy, arthritis, and rheumatism. Surgical procedures have been developed that correct many orthopedic defects and reduce the effects of some neurological dysfunctions.

For many of the individuals who have disabilities, physical therapy is the most important and effective treatment. Through special exercises and therapy, the symptoms of many disabling diseases, such as speech impediments and loss of mobility, can be partially offset. Using special equipment and trained specialists, hospitals and agencies are able to help people with disabilities regain mobility and other bodily functions that have been lost.

Through special education programs, large organizations (such as Easter Seals) and many local agencies teach those who have disabilities how to lead independent, productive lives. These programs range from teaching people who are blind to read braille and use seeing-eye dogs, to showing children with muscular dystrophy how to use their stronger muscles to offset those weakened by disease.

WHAT IS BEING DONE

The federal government spends more than $100 billion a year on programs related to disability. This money is distributed through retirement policies, welfare, the courts system of torts and damages, civil rights policies, and the tax system. Unfortunately, the majority of funds are spent in areas that discourage people with disabilities from seeking rehabilitation, physical therapy and education programs which would enable them to achieve varying degrees of self-sufficiency. About 2% of federal funds goes to rehabilitation, education, and architectural accessibility, while 98% goes to supporting people. In 1984, for example, $1 billion was spent in vocational rehabilitation and on job training and placement programs, while $15.5 billion went to retirement and health benefits in the Social Security Disability Program.

Through the establishment of a federal disability policy and the enactment of Title VII: Comprehensive Services for Independent Living some progress has been made. Successes in recent years include wheelchair accessibility on some public transportation lines, increased special education programs in public schools for students who are mentally and emotionally disabled, special simultaneous sign language translation on some television shows, and sound-indication devices on some street lights. Although prejudice still exists in the workplace, a number of companies have acquired special equipment for people with disabilities to make their jobs easier, such as sensor-operated wheelchairs for easier mobility, computers and other electronic devices that can be operated without the use of hands, and an ultrasonic orientation and navigational device for use by people who are blind and/or deaf.

There have also been positive developments in the ways the media portrays individuals with disabilities. Television shows, such as "L.A. Law" which features Bennie, a mail clerk who is mentally retarded, portray those with mental disabilities as reliable and effective workers. The Oscar award-winning movie, *Rain Man*, starring Dustin Hoffman as a man suffering from autism, showed not only the humanity of people who have mental disabilities, but also the positive emotional impact and increased self-awareness they bring to others around them.

WHAT YOU CAN DO

Although professionals are needed in many areas, such as health care, physical therapy, and legal appeal, untrained volunteers can help provide invaluable assistance in programs for education and therapy, counseling, recreation, respite and family support, as well as fundraising, advocacy and office work. Through their efforts, volunteers can help erase the notion that people with disabilities are or should be separate from the rest of society.

Therapy and Education Programs

Most of these programs are designed to teach and assist people with disabilities to function normally in society. Work can range from training a child with muscular dystrophy in motor skills to teaching language skills to an adult who is autistic or has communication disorders. To foster self-sufficiency, many agencies offer living skills programs to teach disabled adults how to live independently. Other programs have established occupational training to prepare them for employment.

One local program, Little Friends, provides vocational, educational and residential care to 600 children and adults with men-

Pearl: A Volunteer for Children With Disabilities

Pearl's volunteering work as a counselor for children with disabilities began when she offered to help take care of Scotty, her neighbor's seven-month-old boy who had been born with cerebral palsy. Scotty's parents couldn't afford to take time off from work to take him to the county's Early Intervention Program, so Pearl offered. "I didn't think of it as volunteering," says Pearl, "because I was helping a friend."

The Early Intervention Program serves children up to three years of age with developmental problems. The focus is on home-based work, teaching parents to work with the children and get more response from them. One particularly effective and popular program takes place in a nearby pool, which is donated once a week to the group. Volunteers like Pearl work with the kids in the pool, helping them with their specific needs. This has proven especially successful with children with muscle problems. "If a child can't open his hands, for example," says Pearl, "a volunteer will play with him, doing exercises to help him gain better control over his hand muscles."

When Scotty got too old for the program, Pearl still wanted to continue, so she "adopted" another child. That was nine years ago, and since then she has helped over ten children.

tal and physical disabilities. Through a series of programs run in numerous locations around the Chicago area, Little Friends teaches living skills and job training to adults, and offers special schools for children with disabilities. Their volunteer corp of over 175 people provides assistance in all aspects of the programs.

Organizations for the blind, such as Recording for the Blind and the Lighthouse for the Blind, assist people with visual impairments by allowing them access to recorded material and teaching them how to function in society. Using volunteers, Recordings for the Blind has recorded over 70,000 books on all types of subject matters.

Other national organizations, such as Easter Seals, Goodwill Industries, Catholic Charities, and the United Cerebral Palsy Association also run educational and vocational programs for people with disabilities. Across the country, Easter Seals and Catholic Charities provide residential and learning centers that offer vocational exposure and individual instruction geared toward increasing the living skills of people who have disabilities. The United Cerebral Palsy Association has counseling, independent living skills training, and job training. Goodwill Industries offers a vocational rehabilitation program that trains people with disabilities for jobs in data entry, office administration, and food service.

Many school districts across the country have special education classes for students who are mentally and emotionally disabled. The schools use volunteers to give these students individualized attention.

The need for volunteers to work in these programs is great. Volunteers with particular occupational skills, such as computer operation, accounting, retailing, or office administration, can help in vocational training programs. People with counseling or medical backgrounds can be of help in programs that teach independent living skills or in special education or rehabilitation programs. Others can assist teachers and therapists perform clerical or advocacy work or do fundraising.

Counseling Programs

People with disabilities frequently need someone to talk to about the difficulties of being disabled. Counseling programs give individuals with disabilities an outlet to discuss the pain and feelings of separation many of them experience. Volunteers, working with counseling professionals, give needed understanding and love, either one-on-one or in group settings.

Recreational Programs

People with mental or physical disabilities often do not have the opportunity to participate in sports or other recreational activities to the extent that their non-handicapped peers do. Programs have been established so that with assistance people with disabilities can enjoy more activities. One San Francisco organization, Recreation Center for the Handicapped, runs year-round recreational and camping programs. The Center maintains a gym and swimming pool for use by those with disabilities, and maintains and organizes arts and crafts classes and group excursions. Volunteers are used to organize activities, assist participants and teach recreational skills.

THE LITTLE FRIENDS VOLUNTEERS

Little Friends is an independent, not-for-profit agency outside of Chicago that caters to the needs of developmentally disabled children and adults. Jean Morris, Coordinator of Volunteer Services, recently paid tribute to the 175 volunteers who provided a total of 16,800 hours of service to the organization last year. Her remarks highlight the importance of volunteers and the work they do:

> Little Friends volunteers are amazing people. They are high school students who spend five weeks of their summer vacation volunteering in the classrooms at Little Friends School or assisting students one-to-one at Centennial Beach. They are men and women, employed during the day, who make time evenings and weekends to volunteer at the CLF, the CRAs and the Group Home. They are adults who provide classroom assistance at the school, extra hands at PIP and one-to-one training in independent living skills at Spectrum. They are the men and women who staff two Serendipity resale shops six days a week throughout the year accepting, sorting, pricing and selling clothing and household items donated by the public. They are bicycle fixers, party givers, menders, grocery shoppers and baby sitters. They are wonderful!

Volunteers are also needed for athletic programs for people with disabilities. While the Special Olympics is the most widely known event, countless other competitive and noncompetitive programs exist nationwide. Basketball leagues, ski teams, and golf and swimming programs for the disabled abound. One Organization, The Cooperative Wilderness Outdoor Group, even takes disabled persons dog sledding and river rafting. Of course, all of these programs depend on volunteers to coach or help assist the participants.

Respite and Family Support Programs

Families who care for children or adults who are severely disabled are under tremendous stress. Because of the constant care and attention required, family members have to make major sacrifices in their own lives. To help them deal with the emotional stress and to have some time for themselves, support and respite programs have been established across the country. The National Multiple Sclerosis Society offers counseling for family members and runs a respite program, which accepts children with disabilities into its recreational program, which can run for as long as a few weeks. Family Friends matches elderly volunteers with families who are caring for a child with severe disabilities. The volunteer helps care for the child and provides emotional support to the parents, giving them a few hours of free time to themselves.

Advocacy

National organizations, such as Easter Seals, the Multiple Sclerosis Society, the Association of Retarded Persons (ARP), and the United Cerebral Palsy Association, are leading advocates for people who have disabilities. Through lobbying, these organizations push for legislative, occupational and social change to improve the plight of the large segment of the American population that is disabled. For instance, the ARP, through its National Employment and Training Program, works with a nationwide network of employment agencies to help people who are mentally retarded get jobs. The National Easter Seals Society works with hundreds of other organizations, from the Lion's Club to college fraternities and sororities, to advocate and raise funds for programs for people with disabilities. Volunteers can help in many ways, such as answering phones during telethons, participating in letter-writing campaigns, doing office work, and assisting in fundraising events.

HELPING PEOPLE WITH DISABILITIES

Numbering nearly 15% of the nation's population, people who have disabilities are indeed the nation's largest minority. Volunteers have the opportunity to help them overcome the handicaps placed on them by society and help them learn to live successfully with their disabilities. Scores of voluntary organizations around the country desperately need your help.

PART III

Agency Directory

NATIONAL DIRECTORY

Below are descriptions of selected national not-for-profit agencies that have local or regional offices that use volunteers.

ACTION
National Headquarters
Washington, D.C. 20525
800-424-8580

Purpose
Federal Domestic Volunteer Agency. Supports, promotes and recognizes volunteerism in America.

Services
Programs include Foster Grandparent Program, Young Volunteers in Action, Senior Companion Program, Volunteer Drug Use Prevention Program, and more.

Volunteer Needs
Vary according to program and location. One example: the Foster Grandparent program matches companions with children who have special or exceptional needs, such as physical handicaps or a history of abuse or neglect. To qualify, volunteers must be age 60 or older, qualify financially for the modest stipend provided to offset expenses like transportation, and commit to spending 20 hours each week with their "foster" family.

American Association of Retired Persons
National Headquarters
1909 K Street, N.W.
Washington, D.C. 20049
202-728-4248

Purpose
Four goals set forth by its founder: "To enhance the quality of life for older persons; to promote independence, dignity and purpose for older persons; to lead in determining the role and place of older persons in society; and to improve the image of aging."

Services
Several, including: life-enhancing programs in areas such as caregiving, crime prevention, legal rights, and employment; informative publications, television and audio-visual programs; research, communication,

education and advocacy on local, national and international levels; and more.

Volunteer Needs
Policymakers, advisors, managers, educators, advocates, and providers of support and assistance in AARP programs.

Association of Retarded Citizens
National Headquarters
2501 Avenue J
Arlington, Texas 76006
817-640-0204

Purpose
Dedicated to improving the quality of life of people with mental retardation, preventing this handicapping condition, and searching for cures.

Services
Programs serving retarded citizens in the areas of education, job training and placement, independent living and personal fulfillment. Also, programs to assist families, organizations and communities in meeting the needs of people with mental retardation.

Volunteer Needs
Individuals to get involved in citizen advocacy programs, recreational activities, public education, employment programs, etc.

Big Brothers and Big Sisters of America
National Headquarters
Big Brothers/Big Sisters of Philadelphia
230-A N. 13th Street
Philadelphia, Pennsylvania 19105

Services
Professionally supervised friendships between a mature adult and a child who benefits from the guidance and examples set by the adult.

Volunteer Needs
Concerned, responsible men and women to serve ad Big Brothers and Big Sisters, speakers, etc.

Boys Clubs of America
771 First Avenue
New York, New York 10017
212-351-5900

Purpose
The Boys and Girls Club Movement is a national affiliation of local auto-

nomous organizations and Boys Clubs working to help youth of all backgrounds, with special concern for those from disadvantaged circumstances, develop the qualities needed to become responsible citizens and leaders.

Services
Career exploration, health and physical fitness, delinquency prevention, citizen and leadership development, etc.

Volunteer Needs
Varies with each club or organization. May include coaching, tutoring, art/crafts instruction, career guidance, board support, etc.

Catholic Charities
National Headquarters
1319 F Street, N.W.
Washington, D.C. 20004
202-639-8400

Purpose
Serves those in need, advocates for the poor, and works with others for peace and justice.

Services
"Catholic Charities USA provides leadership and support to its members, who offer numerous services to their communities, ranging from adoption and substance abuse counseling to help for the hungry and homeless."

Volunteer Needs
"While not every local Catholic Charities agency is set up to use volunteers, many rely on volunteers for a variety of services."

Family Service America
National Headquarters
11700 W. Lake Park Drive
Park Place
Milwaukee, Wisconsin 53224
414-359-2111

Purpose
Dedicated to strengthening the family.

Services
A variety of family-related services, including marital counseling, crisis intervention, substance abuse counseling, and more.

Volunteer needs
Member agencies may use volunteers in fundraising, community education, direct service such as drivers or friendly visitors, etc.

Girl Scouts of the U.S.A.
National Headquarters
8 33rd Avenue
New York, New York 10022
212-940-7500

Purpose
A movement that gives girls from all segments of American life a chance to develop their potential to make friends and become a vital part of their community. Based on ethical values, Girl Scouts opens up a world of opportunity for youths working in partnership with adult volunteers.

Services
A continuing adventure in learning that offers a broad range of activities which address their current interests and future roles as women, and which stimulate self-discovery. Girls are introduced to excitement in the worlds of science, the arts, the out-of-doors, and people.

Volunteer needs
Leaders, consultants, board members, staff specialists in child development, administrators, educators, etc.

Goodwill Industries of America
9200 Wisconsin Avenue
Bethesda, Maryland 20814
301-530-6500

Purpose
Provides opportunities for people with disabilities or other hardships to live and work to their fullest potential.

Services
Individual Goodwill offices run a variety of programs, which may include vocational guidance, rehabilitation counseling, socialization activities, and more.

Volunteer Needs
Needs vary at each independently run office, but common positions include friendly visitors, counselors, fund-raisers, day care assistants, etc.

Habitat for Humanity
National Headquarters
1233 Plaines Avenue
Americus, Georgia 31709
912-924-6935

Purpose
Dedicated to providing "a decent house in a decent community for God's people in need."

Services
Habitat builds homes by enlisting donations for materials and volunteers to work on all aspects of building or renovating a house.

Volunteer needs
Workers in all aspects of construction—painting, plumbing, moving. Also administrative support, accounting, public speaking and other positions related to support and promote public awareness.

Laubach Literacy International
Purpose
To reduce illiteracy using volunteer tutors in a one-to-one teaching environment.

Services
They recruit and train volunteers, seek out individuals who need to improve basic reading and writing skills, and coordinate tutoring match-ups. In addition, they work to promote public awareness about the problems of illiteracy.

Volunteer Needs
Tutors, tutor trainers, fund-raisers, advisory board members, child care helpers, drivers, clerical assistants, etc.

Literacy Volunteers of America
National Headquarters
5795 Widewaters Parkway
Syracuse, New York 13214
315-445-8000

Services
Recruit and train volunteers, seek out individuals who need to improve basic reading and writing skills, and coordinate tutoring match-ups. In addition, they work to promote public awareness about the problems of illiteracy.

Volunteer Needs
Tutors, tutor trainers, fund-raisers, advisory board members, child care helpers, drivers, clerical assistants, etc.

Lutheran Volunteer Corps
National Headquarters
1226 Vermont Avenue, N.W.
Washington, D.C. 20005
202-387-3222

Purpose
A ministry of Luther Place Memorial Church, which is located in Washington, D.C.

Services
LVC volunteers work in a variety of urban social justice and human care agencies, such as homeless shelters, neighborhood centers and peace and just organizations. Agencies must be approved by LVC and are located in five cities across the country.

Volunteer Needs
Positions range from direct service to advocacy to policy-making. A full-time, one-year commitment is required. Volunteers receive orientation, placement, training, housing, a subsistence salary, and medical insurance.

National AIDS Network
National Headquarters
2033 M Street, N.W.
Suite 800
Washington, D.C. 20036
202-293-2437

Purpose
"National AIDS Network (NAN) was established to provide direct services to, and be the voice of, community-based AIDS service and education providers — organizations that have responded with compassion and sensitivity to the impact of AIDS on the lives of people in their cities and regions."

Services
Supports over 650 organizations that provide community-based education and services. Also serves as a clearinghouse for information and AIDS-related programs.

Volunteer Needs
Each NAN member service provider uses volunteers differently, depending on the range of the services they provide. These may include "hotlines, 'buddy' programs, counseling, food assistance, HIV antibody testing."

National Coalition for the Homeless
National Headquarters
1439 Rhode Island Avenue, N.W.
Washington, D.C. 20005
202-659-3310

Purpose
Research and advocacy for the rights of the homeless.

Services
Supports legislation to improve and provide shelters, assists and advises shelters throughout the country, central source of information and referral on matters pertaining to homelessness.

Volunteer Needs
Advocates, speakers, shelter workers, etc.

National Coalition for the Prevention of Child Abuse
National Headquarters
P.O. Box 94283
Chicago, Illinois 60690
312-663-3520

Purpose
"[A] volunteer-based organization dedicated to involving all concerned citizens in actions to prevent child abuse...committed to reducing child abuse by at least 20 percent by the end of 1990."

Services
The national office and NCPCA chapters administer programs which address a variety of issues, including public awareness, public education, advocacy, and community-based prevention services.

Volunteer Needs
Individuals to work in community-level NCPCA programs and help implement new programs, or to serve on the national volunteer board of directors.

National Easter Seal Society
National Headquarters
2023 West Ogden Avenue
Chicago, Illinois 60612
312-243-8400

Purpose
Provides direct services to meet rehabilitation needs of persons with disabilities, thereby increasing their self-sufficiency and independence.

Services
Direct services include physical, occupational, and speech-language therapies, vocational evaluation and training, camping and recreation, counseling, screening and prevention efforts, etc. Other services include family support, community program development assistance, and advocacy.

Volunteer needs
Several relating to services shown above. Also, telethon phone-answerers, fund-raisers, drivers for clients, office workers, camp help-ers, etc.

National Mental Health Association
National Headquarters
1021 Prince Street
Alexandria, Virginia 22314-2971

Purpose
Works to protect the rights, empower the lives, and improve the social images of people who suffer from mental illnesses.

Services
Several relating to the support of mental health and people suffering from mental illnesses, including: pursuing national legislative action for development and funding of mental health services and protection of rights; training MHA staff and volunteers for more effective interaction with people with mental illnesses; providing information to the public about mental health, mental illnesses, and related services; and more.

Volunteer Needs
Companions for people of all ages with mental illnesses, helpers to assist their families, and advocates for legislation in the areas of services, research and protection of rights.

National Multiple Sclerosis Society
National Headquarters
205 E. 42nd Street
New York, New York 10017
212-986-3240

Services
Serves individuals with multiple sclerosis and their families through direct service programs, research, and advocacy.

Volunteer needs
Local chapters have varying needs, but may use volunteers in fund-raising, friendly visiting, transportation assistance, community educa-tion, etc.

National School Volunteer Program
National Headquarters
701 N. Fairfax Street, Suite 320
Alexandria, Virginia 22314
703-836-4880

Services
Promotes and coordinates volunteer efforts in schools, acts as liaison between community and school system.

Volunteer Needs
Tutors, teacher's aides, field trip chaperons, and more.

The National Urban League
National Headquarters
500 East 62nd Street
New York, New York 10021
212-310-9000

Purpose
Supports and promotes equal opportunity for minorities.

Services
Housing, job training and placement, research and advocacy for minorities on local, state and national levels, and more.

Volunteer Needs
Advocates, literacy tutors, etc.

Recording for the Blind
National Headquarters
20 Roszel Road
Princeton, New Jersey 08540
609-452-0606

Purpose
Originally founded to help blinded World War II veterans attend college, they are now dedicated to assisting "students at all academic levels, business or professional people — or anyone with a visual, physical or perceptual disability that prevent[s] the reading of standard printed material."

Services
They provide "recorded educational books free on loan to blind and other print-handicapped people," in this country and throughout the world. More than 20,000 borrowers are served each year.

Volunteer Needs
Readers, who must first pass a reading test, and monitors, who follow the text for accuracy and record the reader. All individuals must have completed at least two years of college and commit to at least two hours each week. Training in both reading and monitoring is provided at RFB studios.

The Salvation Army
National Headquarters
799 Bloomfield Avenue
Verona, New Jersey 07044

Purpose
Provides a balance of spiritual and physical support to all people in need. "Aid is given wherever and whenever the need is apparent, without distinction as to race or creed and without demand for adherence, simulated or real, to the principles of the Army."

Services
Several, including: resident alcohol rehabilitation centers; maternity homes and outpatient services for unwed mothers; emergency disaster services; youth outreach programs; senior citizens programs; and more.

Volunteer Needs
Vary depending on the programs offered in your area. May use tutors, youth counselors and recreation leaders, etc.

The United Way
National Headquarters
701 N. Fairfax Street
Alexandria, Virginia 22314-2045

Purpose
Established in Colorado as the Charity Organizations Society, the mission of this international organization is "To increase the organized capacity of people to care for one another."

Services
Several, including: funding and/or administration of over 37,000 human care and social justice agencies (These may be United Way offices, chapters of other nationwide organizations, or one-of-a-kind grass-roots organizations founded by people who recognize health and human care needs in their communities, but don't have the funds or organizations structure to meet them alone); recruiting and training of volunteers; and operation of many Volunteer and Voluntary Action Centers, which are clearinghouses of information on local volunteer opportunities and which may also be sponsored by VOLUNTEER—The National Center.

Volunteer needs
Fund-raising, assessing community needs; recruiting and training other volunteers, offering management and technical help to a wide range of community agencies, etc.

Volunteers In Service To America (VISTA)
National Headquarters
111 Vermont, N.W.
Washington, D.C. 20525

Purpose
VISTA strives to enable low-income people throughout the United States to improve their own lives and living conditions.

Services
Several, including: drug-abuse counseling; literacy training; food distribution; shelters for the homeless; neighborhood revitalization; and more.

Volunteer Needs
Individuals 18 years or older who are willing to make a full-time, year-long commitment to a the VISTA program.

VOLUNTEER—The National Center
National Headquarters
1111 North 19th Street, Suite 500
Arlington, Virginia 22209
703-276-0542

Purpose
"To strengthen the effective involvement of all citizens as volunteers in solving local problems."

Services
Several, including: education, consulting, and other support to several organizations that use volunteers; sponsorship of new projects and activities which promote volunteerism; production of publications on volunteer involvement and administration, including *Voluntary Action Leadership*, a quarterly magazine; and operation of many Voluntary Action Centers across the country, which are clearinghouses of information on local volunteering opportunities and which may also be sponsored by The United Way.

Volunteer Needs
Vary depending on their programs. One example: corporate employees can choose an activity in cooperation with their company's own volunteer program through VOLUNTEER's Workplace Programs Unit, a program which promotes corporate volunteerism by providing assistance and training to interested corporations.

Volunteers of America
National Headquarters
3813 N. Causeway Boulevard
Metairie, Lousiana 70002
504-837-2652

Purpose
"Volunteers of America is a movement for the reaching and uplifting of all people in bringing them to the immediate and active service of God." (Sponsored by The Salvation Army.)

Services
Operation of low-income residences, homeless shelters, alcohol rehabilitation programs, thrift shops, and more.

Volunteer Needs
Thrift shop workers, shelters workers, kitchen servers, etc.

LOCAL
VOLUNTEER CENTERS

Below is listed by state and by city Volunteer Centers that use volunteers.

ALABAMA

United Way Volunteer Center
407 Noble Street
P.O. Box 1122
Anniston, AL 36202
Ph: (205) 236-8229

United Way Volunteer Center
3600 8th Avenue, South
Suite 504
Birmingham, AL 35222
Ph: (205) 251-5131
Fax: (205) 323-8730

The Volunteer Center of
of Margan County
303 Cain Street, N.E.
Suite D
P.O. Box 986
Decatur, AL 35602-0986
Ph: (205) 355-8628

Volunteer Information
and Referral Center
408 West Main
P.O. Box 405
Dothan, AL 36302
Ph: (205) 792-4792

Volunteer Action of
the Eastern Shore
150 South Greeno Road
Suite P
P.O. Box 61
Fairhope, AL 36533
Ph: (205) 928-0509

Volunteer Center of
Huntsville & Madison Co.
1101 Washington Street
Huntsville, AL 35801
Ph: (205) 539-7797

Volunteer Mobile
2504 Dauphin Street, Suite K
Mobile, AL 36606
Ph: (205) 479-0631

Voluntary Action Center/
Information & Referral
2125 East South Blvd.
P.O. Box 11044
Montgomery, AL 36111-0044
Ph: (205) 284-0006

ALASKA

Volunteer Services
341 West Tudor Road
Suite 106
Anchorage, AK 99503-6638
Ph: (907) 562-4483
Fax: (907) 563-0020

Volunteer Action Center
P.O. Box 74396
Fairbanks, AK 99707
Ph: (907) 452-7000

ARIZONA

Volunteer Center of
Maricopa County
1515 E. Osborn
Phoenix, AZ 85014
Ph: (602) 263-9736

Volunteer Center of
  Yavapai County
107 N. Cortez, Room 208
Prescott, AZ 86301
Ph: (602) 776-9908

Volunteer Center
877 S. Alverson
Tucson, AZ 85711
Ph: (602) 327-6207

ARKANSAS

United Way Volunteer
  Action Center
P.O. Box 3257
Little Rock, AR 72203-3257
Ph: (501) 376-4567

CALIFORNIA

Volunteer Center of
  Kern Co., Inc.
601 Chester Avenue
Bakersfield, CA 93301
Ph: (805) 327-9346

Community Action Volunteers
  in Education
W. 2nd. & Cherry Streets
Chico, CA 95929-0750
Ph: (916) 895-5817

Volunteer Center of Contra
  Costa County
1070 Concord Avenue, Suite 100
Concord, CA 94520
Ph: (415) 246-1050

Volunteer Center of Orange
  County - North
2050 Youth Way, Bldg. 2
Fullerton, CA 92635
Ph: (714) 526-3301

Volunteer Center of Nevada County
10139 Joerschke Drive
Grass Valley, CA 95945
Ph: (916) 272-5041

La Mirada Volunteer Center
12900 Bluefield Avenue
La Mirada, CA 90638
Ph: (213) 943-0131

Volunteer Center of
  Los Angeles
West Los Angeles Branch
11646 W. Pico Boulevard
Los Angeles, CA 90064
Ph: (213) 445-4200 X30

Volunteer Center of
  Los Angeles
South Central Branch
8812 South Main Street
Los Angeles, CA 90003
Ph: (213) 753-1315

Volunteer Center of
  Los Angeles
2117 W. Temple Street
3rd Floor
Los Angeles, CA 90026
Ph: (213) 484-2849
Fax: (213) 484-8011

Volunteer Center of
  Los Angeles
East/Northeast Branch
133 N. Sunol Drive
Los Angeles, CA 90063-1429
Ph: (213) 267-1325

Volunteer Center of
  Los Angeles
City Hall Branch, M.S. 936
200 N. Spring Street
Room 100L
Los Angeles, CA 90012
Ph: (213) 485-6984

Volunteer Center Orange
  County, West
15055 Adams St., Suite A
Midway City, CA 92655
Ph: (714) 898-0043
Fax: (714) 891-0121

Volunteer Center Stanislaus
2125 Wylie Drive, #4
Modesto, CA 95355
Ph: (209) 524-1307

Monrovia Volunteer Center
119 W. Palm Avenue
Monrovia, CA 91016-2888
Ph: (818) 357-3797

Volunteer Center of the
Monterey Peninsula
444 Pearl Street, A-24
Monterey, CA 93940
Ph: (408) 373-6177

Volunteer Center of
Napa County, Inc.
1820 Jefferson Street
Napa, CA 94559
Ph: (707) 252-6222
Fax: (707) 963-4222

Volunteer Center of
Alameda County, Inc.
1212 Broadway, Suite 622
Oakland, CA 94612
Ph: (415) 893-6239
Fax: (415) 451-3144

Volunteer Center of
San Gabriel Valley
3301 Thorndale Road
Pasadena, CA 91107
Ph: (818) 792-6118

Volunteers Involved for
Pasadena
234 E. Colorado Blvd.
Suite 508
Pasadena, CA 91101
Ph: (818) 405-4073

Valley Volunteer Center
333 Division Street
Pleasanton, CA 94566
Ph: (415) 462-3570

Volunteer Center of the
Greater Pomona Valley, Inc.
436 W. Fourth Street
Suite 201
Pomona, CA 91766
Ph: (714) 623-1284

Volunteer Center of Riverside
2060 University Avenue, #206
Riverside, CA 92507
Ph: (714) 686-4402

Volunteer Center of Sacramento
8912 Volunteer Lane, #140
Sacramento, CA 95826-3221
Ph: (916) 368-3110

United Way of Salinas Valley
P.O. Box 202
Salinas, CA 93902
Ph: (408) 424-7644

United Way of San Diego
County Volunteer Bureau
4699 Murphy Canyon Road
P.O. Box 23543
San Diego, CA 92123
Ph: (619) 492-2090
Fax: (619) 492-2059

Volunteer Center of
San Francisco
1160 Battery Street, #400
San Francisco, CA 94111
Ph: (415) 982-8999
Fax: (415) 399-9214

The Volunteer Exchange of
Santa Clara Co.
1310 S. Bascom Avenue
Suite B
San Jose, CA 95128-4502
Ph: (408) 286-1126

Volunteer Center of
San Mateo County
436 Peninsula Avenue
San Mateo, CA 94401
Ph: (415) 342-0801

Volunteer Center of
  Marin County, Inc.
70 Skyview Terrace
San Rafael, CA 94903
Ph: (415) 479-5660
Fax: (415) 479-9722

Volunteer Center Orange
  County-Central/South
1000 E. Snata Ana Blvd.
Suite 200
Santa Ana, CA 92701
Ph: (714) 953-5757
Fax: (714) 834-0585

Volunteer Center of
  Santa Cruz County
1110 Emeline Avenue
Santa Cruz, CA 95060
Ph: (408) 423-0554

Volunteer Center of
  Sonoma County
1041 Fourth Street
Santa Rosa, CA 95404
Ph: (707) 573-3399

Voluntary Action Center
P.O. Box 878
So. Lake Tahoe, CA 95731
Ph: (916) 541-2611

San Joaquin Volunteer Center
  of United Way
P.O. Box 1585
Stockton, CA 95201
Ph: (209) 943-0870

Volunteer Center South Bay
  Harbor-Long Beach Areas
1230 Cravens Avenue
Torrance, CA 90501
Ph: (213) 212-5009

Tulare Volunteer Bureau, Inc.
115 South "M" Street
Tulare, CA 93274
Ph: (209) 688-0539

Volunteer Center of
  San Fernando Valley
6851 Lennox Avenue
Van Nuys, CA 91405
Ph: (818) 908-5066

Volunteer Center of
  Victor Valley
15561 Seventh Street
Victorville, CA 92392
Ph: (619) 245-8592

City of Visalia Volunteer
  Services Programs
417 N. Locust
Visalia, CA 93291
Ph: (209) 738-3483
Fax: (209) 627-9155

COLORADO

Center for Information
  & Volunteer Action
400 E. Main Street
Aspen, CO 81611
Ph: (303) 925-7887
Fax: (303) 925-3979

Volunteer Boulder County
3305 N. Broadway, Suite 1
Boulder, CO 80304
Ph: (303) 444-4904

Volunteer Center of
  Mile High United Way
2505 18th Street
Denver, CO 80211-3907
Ph: (303) 433-6060
Fax: (303) 433-8383 X341

Volunteer Resource Bureau
  of UW of Weld Co.
1001 9 Avenue
P.O. Box 1944
Greeley, CO 80632
Ph: (303) 353-4300

CONNECTICUT

UW Volunteer Center of
  Eastern Fairfield Co.
75 Washington Avenue
Bridgeport, CT 06604
Ph: (203) 334-5106

The Volunteer Bureau of
  Greater Danbury
337 Main Street
Danbury, CT 06810
Ph: (203) 797-1154

Voluntary Action Center
  for the Capitol Region, Inc.
United Way Building
99 Woodland Street
Hartford, CT 06105
Ph: (203) 247-2580
Fax: (203) 247-7949

Voluntary Action Center
  of Greater New Haven, Inc.
703 Whitney Avenue
New Haven, CT 06511
Ph: (203) 785-1997

Voluntary Action Center
  of Mid-Fairfield
83 East Avenue
Norwalk, CT 06851
Ph: (203) 852-0850
Fax: (203) 852-9357

Voluntary Action Center
  of SE Connecticut
100 Broadway
Norwich, CT 06360
Ph: (203) 887-2519

The Volunteer Center of
  SW Fairfield County
62 Palmer's Hill Road
Stamford, CT 06902
Ph: (203) 348-7714
Fax: (203) 967-9507

DISTRICT OF COLUMBIA

Vol. Clearinghouse of D.C.
1313 New York Ave., NW #303
Washington, DC 20005
Ph: (202) 638-2664

FLORIDA

Volunteer Services of
  Manatee County, Inc.
1001 3rd Avenue, West
Suite 350
Bradenton, FL 34205
Ph: (813) 746-7117

The Volunteer Center of
  Volusia/Flagler Counties
444 N. Beach Street
P.O. Box 1306
Daytona Beach, FL 32015
Ph: (904) 253-0563

Volunteer Broward
1300 South Andrews Avenue
P.O.Box 22877
Fort Lauderdale, FL 33335
Ph: (305) 522-6761

Voluntary Action Center of
  Lee County, Inc.
2243C McGregor Blvd.
Fort Meyers, FL 33901
Ph: (813) 334-0405

The Volunteer Center of
  Alachua County
220 N. Main Street
P.O. Box 14561
Gainsville, FL 32604
Ph: (904) 378-2552

Volunteer Jacksonville,
  Inc.
1600 Prudential Drive
Jacksonville, FL 32207
Ph: (904) 398-7777

UW of Central Florida
  Volunteer Center
1825 North Gilmore Avenue
P.O. Box 51
Lakeland, FL 33802
Ph: (813) 686-6171
Fax: (813) 688-9296

United Way's Center for
  Voluntarism
600 Brickell Avenue
Miami, FL 33131
Ph: (305) 579-2300
Fax: (305) 579-2212

Volunteer Center of
  Collier County
3770 Tamiami Trail North
Naples, FL 33940
Ph: (813) 649-4747

Volunteer Service Bureau
  of Marion County, Inc.
520 S.E. Fort King
Suite C-1
Ocala, FL 32671
Ph: (904) 732-4771

Volunteer Center of
  Central Fla., Inc.
1900 N. Mills Avenue
Suite 1
Orlando, FL 32803
Ph: (407) 896-0945
Fax: (407) 895-4749

Volunteer Pensacola/
  Voluntary Action Center, Inc.
7 North Coyle Street
Pensacola, FL 32501
Ph: (904) 438-5649

The Volunteer Service Bureau
  of Palm Beach County
3700 N. Broadway
Southeast Bank - 2nd Floor
Riviera Beach, FL 33404
Ph: (407) 881-9503

Volunteer Center of Sarasota
1750 17th Street
Sarasota, FL 34234
Ph: (813) 366-0013

Volunteer Action Center
5200 16th Street, N.
P.O. Box 13087
St. Petersburg, FL 33733
Ph: (813) 527-7300
Fax: (813) 527-1646

United Way Volunteer Center
P.O. Box 362
Stuart, FL 34995
Ph: (407) 220-1717

Volunteer Tallahassee, Inc.
307 East Seventh Avenue
Tallahassee, FL 32303
Ph: (904) 222-6263

Volunteer Center of
  Hillsborough County
4023 N. Armenia Avenue
Suite 300
Tampa, FL 33607
Ph: (813) 878-2500

Volunteer Center South
101 W. Venice Avenue
Suite 25
Venice, FL 34285
Ph: (813) 484-4305

GEORGIA

Voluntary Action Center
  of United Way
500 N. Slappey Boulevard
P.O. Box 3609
Albany, GA 31706
Ph: (912) 883-6700

Volunteer Resource Center
P.O. Box 2692
Atlanta, GA 30371
Ph: (404) 527-7346
Fax: (404) 527-7444

Help Line
630 Ellis Street
Augusta, GA 30902
Ph: (404) 826-4460

Voluntary Action Center
Hand-Up, Inc.
206 Pine Street, S.W.
P.O. Box 631
Calhoun, GA 30703
Ph: (404) 629-7283

The Volunteer Center
1425 3rd Avenue
P.O. Box 1157
Columbus, GA 31902
Ph: (404) 596-8657

Voluntary Action Center
of Northwest Georgia
305 S. Thornton Avenue
Suite 2
Dalton, GA 30720
Ph: (404) 226-4357

Volunteer Gainsville
P.O. Box 1193
Gainsville, GA 30503
Ph: (404) 535-5445

Volunteer Macon
2484 Ingleside Avenue, A103
Macon, GA 31204
Ph: (912) 742-6677

Voluntary Action Center
of United Way
P.O. Box 9119
Savannah, GA 31412
Ph: (912) 234-1636

Volunteer Thomasville
144 W. Jackson Street
P.O. Box 1540
Thomasville, GA 31799
Ph: (912) 228-3190 X647

HAWAII

Voluntary Action Center
Of Oahu
200 N. Vineyard Boulevard
Room 603
Honolulu, HI 96817
Ph: (808) 536-7234

IDAHO

United Way Volunteer
Connection
1975 Broadway, Suite B
Boise, ID 83706
Ph: (208) 345-7777

ILLINOIS

The Volunteer Center of
NW Suburban Chicago
306 W. Park Street
Arlington Heights, IL 60005
Ph: (312) 398-1320

The Volunteer Center
560 W. Lake Street
Chicago, IL 60606-1499
Ph: (312) 906-2425
Fax: (312) 876-0721

Volunteer Center of
Knox County
140 E. Main Street
Galesburg, IL 61401
Ph: (309) 343-4434

Volunteer Center of the
Greater Quad Cities
1417 6th Avenue
Moline, IL 61265
Ph: (309) 764-6804

United Way Volunteer Center
1802 Woodfield Drive
Box 44
Savoy, IL 61874
Ph: (217) 352-5151
Fax: (217) 352-6494

Community Volunteer Center
Lincoln Land Community
College
Shepherd Road
Springfield, IL 62794-9256
Ph: (217) 786-2289
Fax: (217) 786-2251

Voluntary Action Center
1606 Bethany Road
Sycamore, IL 60178
Ph: (815) 758-3932

DuPage County Division of
Human Services
Volunteer Development Unit
421 N. County Farm Road
Wheaton, IL 60187
Ph: (708) 682-7505

INDIANA

First Call for Help/
Volunteer Services
646 Franklin
P.O. Box 827
Columbus, IN 47202
Ph: (812) 376-0011

Volunteer Action Center
101 NW First Street-Old
Post Office Place
P.O. Box 18
Evansville, IN 47701
Ph: (812) 421-2801
Fax: (812) 421-7474

Volunteer Connection
227 East Washington Blvd.
Suite 303A
Fort Wayne, IN 46802
Ph: (219) 420-4263

The Window Community
Volunteer Center
223 S. Main Street
Goshen, IN 46526
Ph: (219) 533-9680

The Human Resource Dept.
of United Way
221 West Ridge Road
Griffith, IN 46319
Ph: (219) 923-2302

Volunteer Action Center
1828 N. Meridian Street
Indianapolis, IN 46202
Ph: (317) 923-1466
Fax: (317) 921-1355

Volunteer Action Center
210 W. Walnut Street
Kokomo, IN 46901-4512
Ph: (317) 457-4481

Greater Lafayette Volunteer
Bureau, Inc.
301 1/2 Columbia Street
Lafayette, IN 47901
Ph: (317) 742-8241

Community Resource Center of
St. Joseph County, Inc.
914 Lincolnway West
South Bend, IN 46616
Ph: (219) 232-2522

Volunteer Action Center
721 Wabash Avenue, Suite 502
Terre Haute, IN 47807
Ph: (812) 232-8822

IOWA

Volunteer Bureau of
Story County
510 5th Street
Ames, IA 50010
Ph: (515) 232-2736

Volunteer Bureau of
Council Bluffs
40 Pearl Street
Council Bluffs, IA 51503-0817
Ph: (712) 323-1673

*United Way of Central Iowa
  Volunteer Center*
1111 Ninth Street, Suite 300
Des Moines, IA 50314
Ph: (515) 246-6545
Fax: (515) 246-6546

*The Voluntary Action
  Center of Muscatine*
113 Iowa Avenue
Muscatine, IA 52761
Ph: (319) 263-0959

*VAC of the Iowa Great
  Lakes, Inc.*
1713 Hill Avenue
Spirit Lake, IA 51360
Ph: (712) 336-4444

KANSAS

*Volunteer Center of
  Wyandotte County*
710 Minnesota Avenue
P.O. Box 17-1042
Kansas City, KS 66117
Ph: (913) 371-3674

Roger Hill Volunteer Center
P.O. Box 116
Lawrence, KS 66044
Ph: (913) 865-5030

*Volunteer Center of
  Johnson County*
5311 Johnson Drive
Mission, KS 66205
Ph: (913) 432-0766

*Volunteer Center of
  Topeka, Inc.*
4125 Gage Center Drive
Suite 214
Topeka, KS 66604
Ph: (913) 272-8890

United Way Volunteer Center
212 N. Market, Suite 200
Wichita, KS 67202
Ph: (316) 267-1321
Fax: (316) 267-0937

KENTUCKY

*Volunteer Center of
  Frankfort/Franklin Co.,
  Inc.*
401 West Main Street
P.O. Box 183
Frankfort, KY 40602
Ph: (502) 227-7702

*Volunteer Center of the
  Bluegrass*
2029 Bellefonte Drive
Lexington, KY 40503
Ph: (606) 278-6258

The Volunteer Connection
334 East Broadway
P.O. Box 4488
Louisville, KY 40204-0488
Ph: (502) 583-2821

The Volunteer Center
920 Frederica Street
Suite 404
P.O. Box 123
Owensboro, KY 42302
Ph: (502) 683-9161

LOUISIANA

Volunteer Baton Rouge
8776 Bluebonnet Boulevard
Baton Rouge, LA 70810
Ph: (504) 767-1698

*Volunteer Center of
  Lafayette*
P.O. Box 52074
Lafayette, LA 70505
Ph: (318) 233-1006

*Volunteer Center of
SW Louisiana, Inc.*
111 South Ryan, Suite B
Lake Charles, LA 70601
Ph: (318) 439-6109

United Way of NE Louisiana
1300 Hudson Lane, Suite 7
Monroe, LA 71201
Ph: (318) 325-3869

Volunteer & Info. Agency, Inc.
4747 Earhart Blvd., Suite 111
New Orleans, LA 70125
Ph: (504) 488-4636

MAINE

*The Center for Voluntary
Action of Greater Portland*
233 Oxford Street
Portland, ME 04102
Ph: (207) 874-1015
Fax: (207) 874-1007

MARYLAND

*Volunteer Center of
Frederick Co.*
22 S. Market St.
Frederick, MD 21701
Ph: (301) 663-9096

*Anne Arundel County/
Community Services*
Anne Arundel Center North
101 Crain Highway
Suite 505
Glen Burnie, MD 21061
Ph: (301) 787-6880
Fax: (301) 787-0338

*Prince George Voluntary
Action Center, Inc.*
6309 Baltimore Avenue
Suite 305
Riverdale, MD 20737
Ph: (301) 779-9444

*Montgomery County Volunteer
Center*
50 Monroe Street, #400
Rockville, MD 20850
Ph: (301) 217-9100

MASSACHUSETTS

*VAC/United Way of
Massachusetts Bay*
2 Liberty Square
Boston, MA 02109
Ph: (617) 482-8370
Fax: (617) 482-6021

*Volunteer Service Bureau
of Taunton, Inc.*
4 Court Street
P.O. Box 416
Taunton, MA 02780
Ph: (508) 824-3985

*United Way of Central
Massachusetts*
484 Main Street, Suite 300
Worcester, MA 01608
Ph: (508) 757-5631

MICHIGAN

Voluntary Action Center
2301 Platt Road
Ann Arbor, MI 48104
Ph: (313) 971-5852

*Volunteer Bureau of
Battle Creek*
182 W. Van Buren Street
Battle Creek, MI 49017
Ph: (616) 965-0555

*Volunteer Action Center
of Bay County*
1308 Columbus Avenue
Bay City, MI 48708
Ph: (517) 893-6060

The Center for Volunteerism/
UCS
1212 Griswold at State
Detroit, MI 48226-1899
Ph: (313) 226-9429

Volunteer Center of
United Way
202 E. Boulevard Drive
Room 110
Flint, MI 48503
Ph: (313) 232-8121

Volunteer Center/UW of
Kent County
500 Commerce Building
Grand Rapids, MI 49503-3165
Ph: (616) 459-6281

VAC of Greater Kalamazoo
709-A Westnedge
Kalamazoo, MI 49007
Ph: (616) 382-8350

Voluntary Action Center of
Greater Lansing
6035 Executive Drive
Executive Building
Suite 105
Lansing, MI 48911
Ph: (517) 887-8004

Voluntary Action Center of
Midland County, Inc.
17 Strosacker Center
220 W. Main Street
Midland, MI 48640-5137
Ph: (517) 631-7660

Southwestern Michigan
Volunteer Center
1213 Oak Street
Niles, MI 49120
Ph: (616) 683-5464

Voluntary Action Center
of Saginaw County
118 E. Genesee
Saginaw, MI 48607
Ph: (517) 755-2822

MINNESOTA

Bemidji Area Volunteer
Center
300 Bemidji Avenue
Bemidji, MN 56616
Ph: (218) 759-2802

Voluntary Action Center
402 Ordean Building
424 W. Superior Street
Duluth, MN 55802
Ph: (218) 726-4776

United Way's Voluntary
Action Center
404 South 8th Street
Minneapolis, MN 55404
Ph: (612) 340-7532
Fax: (612) 340-7675

The Volunteer Connection,
Inc.
903 W. Center, Suite 200
Rochester, MN 55902
Ph: (507) 287-2244

Voluntary Action Center of
the St. Paul Area
251 Starkey Street
Sutie 127, Bolander Building
St. Paul, MN 55107
Ph: (612) 227-3938

Community Volunteer Service
of the St. Croix Valley Area
115 So. Union Street
Stillwater, MN 55082
Ph: (612) 439-7434

MISSISSIPPI

Volunteer Center of United Way
843 N. President Street
P.O. Box 23169
Jackson, MS 39225-3169
Ph: (601) 354-1765

Volunteer Jackson County
3510 Magnolia Street
P.O. Box 97
Pascagoula, MS 39567
Ph: (601) 762-7662

MISSOURI

Voluntary Action Center
111 South Ninth
200 Strollway Centre
Columbia, MO 65201
Ph: (314) 449-6959

Voluntary Action Center of
Eastern Jackson County
10901 Winner Road, Suite 102
Independence, MO 64052
Ph: (816) 252-2636

Volunteer Center-Heart of
America United Way
605 West 47th Street
Suite 300
Kansas City, MO 64112
Ph: (816) 531-1945
Fax: (816) 931-8725 X203

Voluntary Action Center
401 N. 12th Street
P.O. Box 188
St. Joseph, MO 64502-0188
Ph: (816) 364-2381

United Way of Greater
St. Louis VAC
1111 Olive
St. Louis, MO 63101
Ph: (314) 421-0700
Fax: (314) 539-4154

MONTANA

Community Help Line
113 6th Street N.
Great Falls, MT 59401
Ph: (406) 761-6010

NEBRASKA

United Way of the Midlands
Volunteer Bureau
1805 Harney St.
Omaha, NE 68102
Ph: (402) 342-8232 X531
Fax: (402) 342-7402

Scotts Bluff County
Volunteer Bureau
1721 Broadway, Room 409
Scottsbluff, NE 69361
Ph: (308) 632-3736

NEVADA

United Way Volunteer Bureau
1055 E. Tropicana, #300
Las Vegas, NV 89119
Ph: (702) 798-4636
Fax: (702) 798-9415

VAC/United Way of
No. Nevada
500 Ryland Street
P.O. Box 2730
Reno, NV 89505-2730
Ph: (702) 322-8668
Fax: (308) 632-3736

NEW HAMPSHIRE

Monadnock Volunteer Center
331 Main Street
Keene, NH 03431
Ph: (603) 352-2088

The Voluntary Action Center
102 N. Main Street
Manchester, NH 03102
Ph: (603) 668-8601

NEW JERSEY

The Volunteer Center of
Camden County
CPAC/HSC
7th & Linden Streets
Camden, NJ 08102
Ph: (609) 541-3939

Volunteer Center of
  Bergen County
64 Passaic Street
Hackensack, NJ 07601
Ph: (201) 489-9454

Volunteer Center of
  Mercer County
3131 Princeton Pike, Bldg. #4
Lawrenceville, NJ 08648
Ph: (609) 896-1912
Fax: (609) 895-1245

Voluntary Action Center of
  Morris County
36 South Street
Morristown, NJ 07960
Ph: (201) 538-7200

Volunteer Center of
  Greater Essex Co., Inc.
303-309 Washington Street
5th Floor
Newark, NJ 07102
Ph: (201) 622-3737

Volunteer Center of
  Atlantic County
P.O. Box 648
Northfield, NJ 08225
Ph: (609) 646-5528

Volunteer Action Center of
  Passaic County
2 Market Street
Paterson, NJ 07501
Ph: (201) 279-8900
Fax: (201) 279-0059

Volunteer Center of
  Monmouth County
188 East Bergen Place
Red Bank, NJ 07701
Ph: (201) 741-3330

Volunteer Center of
  Somerset County
205 W. Main Street
4th Floor
P.O. Box 308
Somerville, NJ 08876-0308
Ph: (201) 725-6640

NEW MEXICO

The Volunteer Center of
  Albuquerque
302 Eight Street, NW
P.O. Box 1767
Albuquerque, NM 87103
Ph: (505) 768-1077

Volunteer Involvement
  Service
LaSalle B-108
College of Santa Fe
Santa Fe, NM 87501
Ph: (505) 473-1000

NEW YORK

The Volunteer Center of
  Albany, Inc.
340 First Street
Albany, NY 12206
Ph: (518) 434-2061

Voluntary Action Center
Vestal Parkway E. at
Jensen Rd.
P.O. Box 550
Binghamton, NY 13902
Ph: (607) 729-2592

Vol. Ctr. of the UW of
  Buffalo/Erie Co.
742 Delaware Avenue
Buffalo, NY 14209
Ph: (716) 887-2626
Fax: (716) 882-0071

The Volunteer Connection
22 W. 3rd Street
P.O. Box 95
Corning, NY 14830
Ph: (607) 936-3753
Fax: (607) 936-0537

Nassau County VAC
320 Old Country Road
Garden City, NY 11530
Ph: (516) 535-3897

Voluntary Action Center, Inc.
65 Ridge St.
Glens Falls, NY 12801
Ph: (516) 793-3817

Voluntary Action Center of
  Suffolk County
90 High Street
Huntington, NY 11743
Ph: (516) 549-1867

Volunteer Service Bureau
  c/o United Way of
  S. Chautauqua Co.
101 East 4th St.
P.O. Box 1012
Jamestown, NY 14701
Ph: (716) 483-1562

Mayor's Vol. Action Center
61 Chambers Street
New York, NY 10007
Ph: (212) 566-5950
Fax: (212) 406-3587

United Way Volunteer
  Connection
55 St. Paul Street
Rochester, NY 14604
Ph: (716) 454 2770
Fax: (716) 454-6568

Volunteer Center, Inc. of
  Syracuse Onondaga Co.
115 E. Jefferson Street
Suite 300
Syracuse, NY 13202
Ph: (315) 474-7011
Fax: (315) 479-6772

Volunteer Center of
  Rensselaer County
502 Broadway
Troy, NY 12180
Ph: (518) 272-1000

Voluntary Action Center
  of Greater Utica, Inc.
1644 Genesee Street
Utica, NY 13502
Ph: (315) 735-4463

Volunteer Service Bureau
  of Westchester
470 Mamroneck Avenue
White Plains, NY 10605
Ph: (914) 948-4452

Rome Voluntary Action Center
City Hall on the Mall
Rome, NY 13440
Ph: (315) 336-5638

Volunteer Center of the
  Human Scvs. Planning Council
152 Barrett Street
Schenectady, NY 12305
Ph: (518) 372-3395

NORTH CAROLINA

Volunteer Service Bureau
50 S. French Broad Avenue
Asheville, NC 28801
Ph: (704) 255-0696

UW/Voluntary Action Center
301 South Brevard Street
Charlotte, NC 28202
Ph: (704) 372-7170
Fax: (704) 342-4482

*Voluntary Action Center of
    Greensboro, Inc.*
1301 N. Elm Street
Greensboro, NC 27401
Ph: (919) 373-1633

*Volunteer Center of Vance
    County, Inc.*
414 S. Garnett Street
P.O. Box 334
Henderson, NC 27536
Ph: (919) 492-1540

Volunteer Center
475 South Church Street
P.O. Box 487
Hendersonville, NC 28793
Ph: (704) 692-8700

*Volunteer Center of
    Greater High Point*
Holt McPherson Center
305 N. Main Street
High Point, NC 27260
Ph: (919) 883-6171
Fax: (919) 883-6928

*Dare Voluntary Action
    Center, Inc.*
P.O. Box 293
Manteo, NC 27954-0293
Ph: (919) 473-2400

*United Way of Wake Co.
    Voluntary Action Center*
1100 Wake Forest Road
P.O. Box 11426
Raleigh, NC 27511
Ph: (919) 833-5739

*United Way of Cleveland
    County, Inc.*
P.O. Box 2242
Shelby, NC 28150
Ph: (704) 482-7344

*Volunteer & Information
    Center*
P.O. Box 333
Supply, NC 28462
Ph: (919) 754-4766

*Voluntary Center of Greater
    Durham, Inc.*
119 Orange Street
Durham, NC 27701
Ph: (919) 688-8977

*The Cumberland County
    Voluntary Action Center,
    Inc.*
P.O. Box 2001
Fayetteville, NC 28302
Ph: (919) 323-8643

*Volunteer Center-United
    Way*
311 W. 4th Street
Winston-Salem, NC 27101
Ph: (919) 723-3601
Fax: (919) 724-1045

NORTH DAKOTA

*Missouri Slope Areawide
    United Way*
P.O. Box 2111
Bismarck, ND 58502
Ph: (701) 255-3601

United Way of Cass-Clay
315 N. Eighth Street
P.O. Box 1609
Fargo, ND 58107-1609
Ph: (701) 237-5050

United Way/Community
Services
323 1/2 De Mers Avenue
P.O. Box 207
Grand Forks, ND 58206-0207
Ph: (701) 775-0671

OHIO

The Volunteer Center
500 West Exchange Street
Akron, OH 44302
Ph: (216) 762-8991

Voluntary Action Center/
A Service of United Way
618 Second Street, NW
Canton, OH 44703
Ph: (216) 453-9172

Info-Line/Volunteer Bureau
107 Water Street
Chardon, OH 44024
Ph: (216) 729-7931
Fax: (216) 286-3442

VAC/United Appeal &
Community Chest
2400 Reading Road
Cincinnati, OH 45202
Ph: (513) 762-7171

The Volunteer Center/
United Way Services
3100 Euclid Avenue
Cleveland, OH 44115-2577
Ph: (216) 361-1010
Fax: (216) 432-4863

CALLVAC
370 South Fifth Street
Columbus, OH 43215
Ph: (614) 221-6766

Voluntary Action Center of
United Way
184 Salem Avenue
Dayton, OH 45406
Ph: (513) 225-3066
Fax: (513) 225-3074

United Way Voluntary
Action Center
20 N. Mechanic
Lebanon, OH 45036
Ph: (513) 932-3987

Volunteer Lima
c/o Churchpeople for
Change and Reconciliation
326 W. McKibben Street
Lima, OH 45801
Ph: (419) 229-6949

Medina County Organization
on Volunteering
246 Northland Drive
Medina, OH 44256
Ph: (216) 723-9614

Voluntary Action Center of
Erie County, Inc.
158 E. Market Street
Room 610
Sandusky, OH 44870
Ph: (419) 627-0074

Volunteer Service Bureau
616 N. Limestone St.
Springfield, OH 45503
Ph: (513) 322-4262

*United Way/Voluntary
Action Service*
1 Stranahan Square
Suite 141
Toledo, OH 43604
Ph: (419) 244-3063
Fax: (419) 246-4614

The Volunteer Registry
215 S. Walnut Street
Wooster, OH 44691
Ph: (216) 264-9473

OKLAHOMA

Tulsa Volunteer Center
1430 S. Boulder
Tulsa, OK 74119
Ph: (918) 585-5551
Fax: (918) 582-5588

OREGON

*Voluntary Action Center/
YMCA*
2055 Patterson
Eugene, OR 97405
Ph: (503) 686-9622

*Volunteer Bureau of
Greater Portland*
718 West Burnside
Room 404
Portland, OR 97209
Ph: (503) 222-1355

PENNSYLVANIA

*Voluntary Action Center of
the United Way*
520 E. Broad Street
Bethlehem, PA 18018
Ph: (215) 691-6670
Fax: (215) 867-7255

*The Franklin County
Volunteer Center, Inc.*
68 S. 3rd Street
Chambersburg, PA 17201
Ph: (717) 261-1133

*Volunteer Center of
Clearfield County*
c/o Clearfield County Area
Agency on Aging
103 N. Front Street
P.O. Box 550
Clearfield, PA 16830
Ph: (814) 765-1398
Fax: (814) 765-2760

*COVE/Council on Volunteers
for Erie County*
110 West 10th Street
Erie, PA 16501-1466
Ph: (814) 456-6248

The Voulunteer Center
546 Maclay Street
Harrisburg, PA 17110
Ph: (717) 238-6678

*Volunteer Center of
Lancaster County*
630 Janet Avenue
Lancaster, PA 17601
Ph: (717) 299-3743

Volunteer Action Council, Inc.
Seven Benjamin Franklin
Parkaway
Philadelphia, PA 19103
Ph: (215) 568-6360

Volunteer Action Center
United Way of Allegheny County
200 Ross Street
P.O. Box 735
Pittsburgh, PA 15230
Ph: (412) 261-6010
Fax: (412) 394-5376

Voluntary Action Center of
NE Pennsylvania
225 N. Washington Ave.
Scranton, PA 18510
Ph: (717) 347-5616

Voluntary Action Center of
Centre County, Inc.
1524 W. College Avenue, #8
State College, PA 16801-2715
Ph: (814) 234-8222

Clyde J. Tracanna Vol. Res.
Ctr. of Washington Co.
c/o United Way of
Washington Co.
58 East Cherry Avenue
Washington, PA 15301
Ph: (412) 225-3322

Volunteer Action Center
United Way of Wyoming
Valley
9 East Market Street
Wilkes-Barre, PA 18711-0351
Ph: (717) 822-3020

The Volunteer Center of
York County
800 East King St.
United Way Bldg.
York, PA 17403
Ph: (717) 846-4477
Fax: (717) 843-4082

RHODE ISLAND

Volunteers in Action, Inc.
160 Broad Street
Providence, RI 02903
Ph: (401) 421-6547

SOUTH CAROLINA

Western Foothills United
Way Volunteer Center
114 W. Greenville Street
P.O. Box 2067
Anderson, SC 29622
Ph: (803) 226-1078

Volunteer & Info. Center
of Beaufort
706 Bay Street (upstairs)
P.O. Box 202
Beaufort, SC 29901-0202
Ph: (803) 524-4357

VAC-Trident United Way
P.O. Box 20696
Charleston, SC 29413-0696
Ph: (803) 760-6930
Fax: (803) 767-2249

United Way Voluntary Action
Center
1800 Main Street
P.O. Box 152
Columbia, SC 29202
Ph: (803) 733-5400

Volunteer Greenville
301 University Ridge
Suite 5300
Greenville, SC 29601-3672
Ph: (803) 232-6444
Fax: (803) 240-8535

Voluntary Action Center
P.O. Box 4759
Hilton Head Island, SC 29938
Ph: (803) 785-6646

Oconee Volunteer &
Information Services
P.O. Box 1828
Seneca, SC 29679
Ph: (803) 882-9744

United Way of the Piedmont
Volunteer Center
101 East St. John Street
Suite 307
P.O. Box 5624
Spartanburg, SC 29304
Ph: (803) 582-7556
Fax: (803) 582-9826

Volunteer Sumter, Inc.
34 E. Calhoun
P.O. Box 957
Sumtec, SC 29151
Ph: (803) 775-9424

SOUTH DAKOTA

Volunteer & Information
Center
304 S. Phillips, Suite 310
Sioux Falls, SD 57102
Ph: (605) 339-4357

Yankton Volunteer &
Information Center
P.O. Box 851
Yankton, SD 57078
Ph: (605) 665-6067

TENNESSEE

The Volunteer Center
451 River Street
P.O. Box 4029
Chattanooga, TN 37405
Ph: (615) 265-0514

Volunteer-Johnson City
200 E. Main Street
Suite 202
P.O. Box 1443
Johnson City, TN 37605
Ph: (615) 926-8010

Volunteer-East Tennessee
State University
Student Activities Center
P.O.Box 21040A
Johnson City, TN 37614
Ph: (615) 929-5675

Volunteer Kingsport, Inc.
1701 Virginia Avenue
Kingsport, TN 37664
Ph: (615) 247-4511

Vol. Ctr. of UW of Greater
Knoxville, Inc.
1514 East Fifth Avenue
P.O. Box 326
Knoxville, TN 37901-0326
Ph: (615) 523-9135
Fax: (615) 522-7312

Volunteer Center of Memphis
263 S. McLean Boulevard
Memphis, TN 38104
Ph: (901) 276-8655
Fax: (901) 276-5700

Volunteer Center-United Way
of Nashville
250 Venture Circle
Nashville, TN 37228
Ph: (615) 256-8272
Fax: (615) 780-2426

TEXAS

Volunteer Center of
Abilene, Inc.
P.O. Box 3953
Abilene, TX 79604
Ph: (915) 676-5683

The United Way Volunteer
Action Center
2207 Line Avenue
P.O.Box 3069
Amarillo, TX 79116-3069
Ph: (806) 376-6714

Volunteer Resource Center
of Brazoria County
P.O. Box 1959
Angleton, TX 77516-1959
Ph: (409) 849-4404
Fax: (409) 848-0259

Capital Area Volunteer
Center, Inc.
5828 Balcones, Suite 205
Austin, TX 78731
Ph: (512) 451-6651

Volunteer Action Center of
Southeast Texas, Inc.
P.O. Box 2945
Beaumont, TX 77704
Ph: (409) 898-2273

Volunteer Resource Center
1301 Los Ebanos, Suite B-3
Brownsville, TX 78520
Ph: (512) 544-0321

Volunteer Center of the
Coastal Bend
1721 S. Brownlee Boulevard
Corpus Christi, TX 78404
Ph: (512) 887-4543

Volunteer Center of
Dallas County
2816 Swiss
Dallas, TX 75204
Ph: (214) 744-1194
Fax: (214) 821-8716

Volunteer Bureau of
United Way
1918 Texas Street
P.O. Box 3488
El Paso, TX 79923
Ph: (915) 533-2434

Volunteer Center of
Metropolitan Tarrant Co.
210 East Ninth Street
Fort Worth, TX 76102-6494
Ph: (817) 878-0099
Fax: (817) 878-0005

Volunteers In Service
To Others
P.O. Box 607
Gainesville, TX 76240
Ph: (817) 668-6403

The Volunteer Center of
the Texas Gulf Coast
3100 Timmons Lane
Suite 100
Houston, TX 77027
Ph: (713) 965-0031

The Volunteer Center of
Longview
500 E. Whaley Street
Longview, TX 75601
Ph: (214) 758-2374

Volunteer Center of Lubbock
1706 - 23rd Street
Suite 101
Lubbock, TX 79411
Ph: (512) 747-0551

Volunteer Resource
Center, Inc.
2217 Primrose
McAllen, TX 78504
Ph: (512) 630-3003

The Volunteer Center of
Midland
1030 Andrews Highway
Suite 207
P.O. Box 2145
Midland, TX 79702
Ph: (915) 697-8781

Volunteer Center of Plano
301 W. Parker Road
Suite 213
Plano, TX 75023
Ph: (214) 422-1050

United Way Volunteer Center
700 South Alamo
P.O. Box 898
San Atonio, TX 78293-0898
Ph: (512) 224-5000
Fax: (512) 224-4245

Texarkana Volunteer Center
3000 Texas Boulevard
Taxarkana, TX 75503
Ph: (214) 793-4903

*Volunteer Center, A service
of United Way Waco*
201 West Waco Drive
P.O. Box 2027
Waco, TX 76703
Ph: (817) 753-5683

UTAH

Voluntary Action Center
236 North, 100 East
P.O. Box 567
Logan, UT 84321
Ph: (801) 752-3103

*Weber County Volunteer
Center*
2650 Lincoln Avenue, Rm 268
Ogden, UT 84401
Ph: (801) 625-3782

United Way Volunteer Center
60 E. 100 S.
P.O. Box 135
Provo, UT 84603
Ph: (801) 374-8108
Fax: (801) 374-2591

VAC of Community Svcs. Council
212 West 1300 South
Salt Lake City, UT 84115
Ph: (801) 486-2136

VERMONT

Volunteer Connection
United Way of Chittenden
Co.
One Burlington Square
Burlington, VT 05401
Ph: (802) 864-7498

VIRGINIA

Alexandria Volunteer Bureau
801 N. Pitt Street, #102
Alexandria, VA 22314
Ph: (703) 836-2176

*The Arlington Volunteer
Office*
2100 Clarendon Boulevard
#1 Court House Plaza
Suite 314
Arlington, VA 22201
Ph: (703) 358-3222

*Volunteer Center of
Montgomery County*
Corner of W. Roanoke and
Otey Streets
P.O. Box 565
Blacksburg, VA 24063-0565
Ph: (703) 552-4909

Volunteer-Bristol
P.O. Box 1599
Bristol, VA 24203
Ph: (703) 669-1555

United Way Volunteer Center
413 E. Market, Suite 101
P.O. Box 139
Charlottesville, VA 22902
Ph: (804) 972-1705
Fax: (804) 972-1719

*VAC of Fairfax County
Area, Inc.*
10530 Page Avenue
Fairfax, VA 22030
Ph: (703) 246-3460

VAC of the Virginia Peninsula
1520 Aberdeen Road, Suite 109
Hampton, VA 23666
Ph: (804) 838-9770

VAC of United Way of
  Central Virginia
1010 Miller Park Square
P.O. Box 2434
Lynchburg, VA 24501
Ph: (804) 847-8657

Voluntary Action Center of
  the Prince William Area
9300 Peabody Street
Suite 104
Manassas, VA 22110
Ph: (703) 369-5292

VAC of S. Hampton Roads
253 West Freemason Street
Norfolk, VA 23510
Ph: (804) 624-2403

VAC of Southwest Virginia
Route 19, SVCC Training Center
P.O. Box SVCC
Richlands, VA 24641
Ph: (703) 964-4915

VC of UW of Greater Richmond
4001 Fitzhugh Avenue
P.O. Box 6649
Richmond, VA 23230-0649
Ph: (804) 353-2000 X224
Fax: (804) 353-0308

Voluntary Action Center
920 South Jefferson Street
P.O. Box 496
Roanoke, VA 24003
Ph: (703) 985-0131

WASHINGTON

The Volunteer Center
c/o American Red Cross
2111 King Street
Bellingham, WA 98225
Ph: (206) 733-3290

The Volunteer Center-United
  Way of Snohomish County
917-134th Street SW, A-6
Everett, WA 98204
Ph: (206) 742-5911
Fax: (206) 743-1440

Benton-Franklin Volunteer
  Center
205 N. Dennis
Kennewick, WA 99336
Ph: (509) 783-0631

Voluntary Aciton Center
613 South Second
P.O. Box 1507
Mt. Vernon, WA 98273
Ph: (206) 336-6627

Washington State Center
  for Voluntary Action
Ninth and Columbia Building
MS: GH-51
Olympia, WA 98504-4151
Ph: (206) 753-0548

United Way Volunteer Center
  of King County
107 Cherry Street
Seattle, WA 98104
Ph: (206) 461-3751

United Way's Volunteer
  Center
P.O. Box 326
Spokane, WA 99210-0326
Ph: (509) 838-6581

VC of UW of Pierce County
· 734 Broadway
P.O. Box 2215
Tacoma, WA 98401
Ph: (206) 272-4267
Fax: (206) 597-7481

*Volunteer Bureau of Clark
  County*
1703 Main Street
P.O. Box 425
Vancouver, WA 98666
Ph: (206) 694-6577

*Greater Yakima Volunteer
  Bureau*
302 W. Lincoln
Yakima, WA 98902
Ph: (509) 248-4460

WEST VIRGINIA

Volunteer Action Center
1007 Mary Street
Parkersburg, WVA 26101
Ph: (304) 428-6344

WISCONSIN

*Information and Referral
  Center*
120 N. Morrison Street
P.O. Box 1091
Appleton, WI 54911
Ph: (414) 832-6000

*Kenosha Voluntary Action
  Center*
716 - 58th Street
Kenosha, WI 53140
Ph: (414) 657-4554

VAC/United Way of Dane Co.
2059 Atwood Avenue
Madison, wI 53704
Ph: (608) 246-4380
Fax: (608) 246-4349

*Volunteer Center of
  Greater Milwaukee, Inc.*
600 E. Mason Street
Suite 100
Milwaukee, WI 53202
Ph: (414) 273-7887
Fax: (414) 273-0637

Volunteer Service Bureau/VAC
431 Olympian Boulevard
Beloit, WI 53511
PH; (608) 365-1278

Volunteer Center
338 S. Chestnut
Green Bay, WI 54303
Ph: (414) 435-1101

*Volunteer Center of
  Waukesha Co., Inc.*
2220 Silvernail Road
Pewaukee, WI 53072
Ph: (414) 544-0150

*The United Way Volunteer
  Center*
1045 Clark Street, #204
Stevens Point, WI 54481
Ph: (715) 341-6740

*Wausau Area Volunteer
  Exchange*
407 Grant Street
Wausau, WI 54401
Ph: (715) 845-5279

*Volunteer Center of
  Washington County*
120 N. Main Street, #340
West Bend, WI 53095
Ph: (414) 338-8256

WYOMING

*Volunteer Information
  Center*
900 Central
P.O. Box 404
Cheyenne, WY 82003
Ph: (307) 632-4132

CANADA

Volunteer Ontario
2 Dunbloor Road, Suite 203
Etobicoke, Ont., CAN M9A 2E4
Ph: (416) 487-6139
Fax: (416) 487-6160

Moncton Volunteer Centre
  Du Benevolat
236 St. George Street
Suite 406
Moncton, NB, CAN E1C 1W1
Ph: (506) 857-8005

Saint John Volunteer Centre, Inc.
P.O. Box 7091, Sta. A
Saint John, NB, CAN EWL 4S5
Ph: (502) 658-1555
Fax: (502) 633-7724

The Vancouver Volunteer Centre
#301-3102 Main Street
Vancouver, BC, CAN V5T 3G7
Ph: (604) 875-9144

FOR FURTHER READING

Armstrong, Louise. *The Home Front: Notes From the Family War Zone.* New York: McGraw Hill, 1983.

Berkowitz, Edward D. *Disabled Policy: America's Programs for the Handicapped.* Cambridge: Cambridge University Press, 1987.

Chambre, Susan Maizel. *Good Deeds in Old Age.* Lexington, Mass.: Lexington Books, 1987.

Council on Scientific Affairs. "Elder Abuse and Neglect." *JAMA: Journal of the American Medical Association,* February 20, 1987.

Douglas, Paul Harding and Laura Pinsky. *The Essential AIDS Fact Book.* New York: Pocket Books, 1991.

Dychtwald, Ken and Joe Flower. *Age Wave: The Challenges and Opportunities of an Aging America.* Los Angeles: Jeremy P. Tarcher, 1989.

Ellwood, David T. *Poor Support: Poverty in the American Family.* New York: Basic Books, Inc., 1988.

Evans, Glen and Norman Faberow. *The Encyclopedia of Suicide.* New York: Facts on File, 1988.

Ferrill, Lisa. *A Far Cry From Home: Life in a Shelter for Homeless Women.* Chicago: The Noble Press, 1991.

Gartner, Alan and Tom Joe. *Images of the Disabled, Disabling Images.* New York: Praeger Publishers, 1988.

Gelles, Richard J. and Murray A. Straus. *Intimate Violence.* New York: Simon and Schuster, 1988.

Gottlieb, Naomi, ed. *Alternative Social Services for Women.* New York: Columbia University Press, 1980.

Grollman, Earl A. *Suicide: Prevention, Intervention, Postvention.* Boston: Beacon Press, 1988.

INDEPENDENT SECTOR. *Giving and Volunteering in the United States: Findings from A National Survey.* District of Columbia: INDEPENDENT SECTOR, 1988.

Johnson, Julie Tallard. *Hidden Victims: An Eight-stage Healing Process for Families and Friends of the Mentally Ill.* New York: Doubleday, 1988.

Karp, Walter. *Liberty Under Seige: American Politics 1976-1988.* New York: Henry Holt, 1988.

Kleiman, Dena and Bruce Lambert. "The Changing Face of AIDS." Series. *The New York Times,* February 7-8, 1989.

Kozol, Jonathan. "Are the Homeless Crazy?" *Harper's,* September 1988. (First published as "Distancing the Homeless" in *Yale Review,* Winter 1988.)

———. *Illiterate America.* New York: Anchor Press/Doubleday & Company, Inc., 1985.

———. *Rachel and Her Children: Homeless Families in America.* New York: Fawcett Columbine, 1988.

Literacy Volunteers of America. *Tutor,* by Ruth Colvin and Jane Root. Folett Publishing Company, 1987.

Loeser, Herta. Women, Work, and Volunteering. Boston: Beacon Press, *1974.*

Luks, Allan. "Helper's High." *Psychology Today,* October 1988.

Maybanks, Sheila and Marvin Bryce, eds. *Home-Based Services for Children and Families.* Springfield, Ill.: Charles C. Thomas, 1979.

Mayhall, Pamela and Katherine Norgard. *Child Abuse and Neglect: Sharing Responsibility.* New York: MacMillan Publishing Company, 1986.

Margolis, Richard. "Bring Us To This Hovel." *New Leader,* January 13, 1986.

McGuire, Paula. *It Won't Happen To Me: Teenagers Talk About Pregnancy.* New York: Delacorte Press, 1983.

Meier, Joan. "Battered Justice." *The Washington Monthly,* May 1987.

Merton, Thomas. *No Man Is An Island.* New York: Harvest/Harcourt Brace Jovanovich, 1983.

Miller, Bryan. "Love Amid the Rubble." *The Chicago Reader,* November 18, 1988.

Moore, Larry F., ed. *Motivating Volunteers.* Vancouver: The Vancouver Volunteer Centre, 1985.

O'Connell, Brian, ed. *America's Voluntary Spirit.* New York: The Foundation Center, 1983.

Okun, Lewis, *Woman Abuse: Facts Replacing Myths.* Albany: State University of New York, 1986.

Park, Jane Mallory. *Meaning Well Is Not Enough.* South Plainfield, NJ: Groupwork Today, Inc., 1983.

The President's Volunteer Action Awards: 1990, brochure, published by VOLUNTEER—The National Center and ACTION.

Raynolds, John F. and Eleanor Raynolds. *Beyond Success.* New York: Master Media Limited, 1985.

Richards, Keith. *Tender Mercies: Inside the World of a Child Abuse Investigator.* Chicago: The Noble Press, 1991.

Schorr, Lisbeth B. with Daniel Schorr. *Within Our Reach: Breaking the Cycle of Disadvantage.* New York: Anchor Press/Doubleday & Company, Inc., 1988.

Siegel, Jacob. "Demographic Perspectives on the Long-Lived Society." *Daedalus,* Winter, 1986.

Stenzel, Anne K. and Helen M. Feeney. *Volunteer Training and Development.* New York: The Seabury Press, 1968.

Toner, Robin. "Americans Favor Aid for Homeless." *The New York Times*, January 21, 1989.

Torrey, E. Fuller. *Nowhere To Go*. New York: Harper and Row, 1988.

U.S. Department of Health and Human Services. "Child Abuse and Neglect: A Shared Community Concern." March 1989.

————. "Surgeon General's Report on Acquired Immune Deficiency Syndrome."

Wilson, William Julius. *The Truly Disadvantaged: the Inner City, the Underclass, and Public Policy*. Chicago: The University of Chicago Press, 1987.

Wright, James D. "The Worthy and Unworthy Homeless." *Society*, July/August 1988.

INDEX

ABOUT THE AUTHOR

DAVID DRIVER knows first-hand the benefits of volunteering, having been both a volunteer and a recipient of its goodwill. Growing up on public aid on Chicago's West Side, Driver and his family were dependent on the charity of local volunteer agencies to get by. Through the help and guidance of volunteer workers, counselors, and Boy Scout troop leaders, Driver was encouraged to stay in school and avoid the gangs and drugs that were prevalent in his neighborhood.

Driver attended Bradley University. After graduating, he began a career as an account executive at Merrill Lynch while pursing his MBA at the University of Chicago. He went on to become a Merrill Lynch Vice President and the firm's most successful institutional financial futures trader.

Driver began his volunteer work while at Bradley, serving as a tutor to inner-city youths. Since that time he has volunteered as a mentor and tutor for youths in Chicago, and has also volunteered at a homeless shelter and at a home for abused children. During 1990, Driver also served as the Resource Chairman for the Association of Volunteer Administrators.

Currently, Driver stays busy as president of The Noble Press, Inc., a publishing company he founded that is dedicated to producing books on social issues; as an employment training volunteer at Jobs for Youth; and as Recruitment Chairman for the United Way of Chicago's Volunteer Center.